Other Books By The Author:

Co-author, *The Computer Art Book* (W.W. Norton & Co.)

Computer Law Forms Handbook (Clark Boardman & Co.)

Lindey On Entertainment, Publishing and the Arts, vol. 3, *Computers* (Clark Boardman & Co.)

Jews and the American Revolution (McFarland & Co.)

What You Aren't Supposed To Know About Writing And Publishing (Shapolsky Publishers, Inc.)

Screenplays By The Author:

Carthage (Corporation for Public Broadcasting)

A Poet Of His People (Corporation for Public Broadcasting)

WHAT YOU AREN'T SUPPOSED TO KNOW ABOUT THE LEGAL PROFESSION

AN EXPOSÉ OF LAWYERS, LAW SCHOOLS, JUDGES AND MORE

An Insider's Report

By

LAURENS R. SCHWARTZ

Shapolsky Publishers, Inc.
New York

126386

Disclaimer: Except for public figures or events, no names are mentioned in this book. The lawyers, judges, and other persons discussed herein are composites based upon actual experiences of the author, and information provided to him by others in the law. Portions of this book are satirical, but the book in its entirety is based upon factual truth and reasoned opinion.

Library of Congress Cataloging-in-Publication Data
Schwartz, Laurens R.
What you aren't supposed to know about the legal profession: an exposé of lawyers, law schools, judges and more / by Laurens R. Schwartz -- 1st ed.
    p.   cm.

Cloth ISBN 0-944007-02-3
Paperback ISBN 1-56171-023-7

1. Law partnership -- United States -- Popular works. 2. Law firms -- United States -- Popular works. 3. Practice of law -- United States -- Popular works.
I. Title.
KF300.Z9S35 1988
340' .023'73--dc19   88-16910

Printed and bound by Graficromo s.a., Cordoba, Spain

Dedicated to all the decent, intelligent lawyers and judges who never make the news

TABLE OF CONTENTS

INTRODUCTION

This book is intended for law students, lawyers, judges, corporate counsel, actual and potential clients, and the public at large. The primary emphasis is on "high powered" law, as opposed to the small town or laid back law that is practiced in many areas of the country. But this book has certain practical aspects that could help a law student or associate become a partner, just as it tries to give insights to clients in terms of saving money when legal problems arise. Overall, the book is a composite of experiences I have had working in the law department of a corporation and as an associate at two prestige firms, plus the experiences of the hundreds of other attorneys I have met during the course of my practice.

I am not mentioning specific names in this book primarily because the legal community has no sense of humor when it comes to poking fun at itself, as opposed to making fun of everyone else, particularly associates passed over for partnership after having been promised partnership, clients who pay outrageous fees, and wives who support their husbands through law school prior to divorce.

The odds are that you will recognize many of the situations I am going to detail, or that you will nod your head without surprise at some of the facts I am going to state. I suspect that the legal community will rear its shaggy head and contend that nothing said in this book is true or, if so, that it represents only a small part of the practice of law. Lawyers like to hide behind the shield known as professionalism and insist that whereas everyone else is amoral, they ride forth on a banner of intellectual honesty and ethics.

Caveat:[1] My years in the law have served to drastically curtail my writing ability. Legal writing is a tortured form of redundancy, hyperbole, and idiocy. Moreover, legal documents are never shorter than a hundred pages because of a major linguistic concept known as Billing. That is why this book is a book instead of the postcard it was intended to be. For those of you who already write lengthy, nonsen-

1

sical pieces that other people buy, there is no hope for you, for you will undoubtedly become partners within four years of graduation from law school.

Since structure is extremely important to the law as one of its primary superficial cements, let me briefly outline this book even though it is outlined in the Table of Contents. As pointed out in the Table of Contents, I will begin with the genetic structure of lawyers. That will be a highly technical discourse requiring referral to a magistrate who, if he does not have degrees in biochemistry and genetic engineering, must at least be distantly related to a judge. For those of you who have no genes, skip that part.

The next chapter, and I again refer the reader to the clear wording of the Table of Contents which also happens to list paginations and to be in type no smaller in size than 8-point, gets into the nitty gritty of education. The major emphasis will be on law school and related matters, such as LSAT scores, grades, law review, moot court, drinking, and the proper manner of socializing (including a brief dissertation on birth control and appropriate hot lines available twenty-four hours a day).

The rest of this book will involve a discussion of life in a law firm, life in a corporation, and life in a courthouse. Without doubt, it is essential, as will be convincingly proven in this book, that a fledgling attorney wishing to live a long and healthy life not make it in a law firm. And, as will be in any event shown, those who make it against their wills will indisputably have something to chuckle about when they have become one of those elderly persons who can always be found in most firms, wandering the hallways late at night muttering to themselves.

Conclusions

The conclusions have been placed here so that you can test whether they have any relation to what the book later declares. The genetic lawyer knows that memoranda have their conclusions in the front of the memo (and sometimes also in the rear, where rational

A TYPICAL EXHIBIT
(THIS IS A CONTRACT, OR LEASE, OR SOMETHING)

people might expect them).

As pointed out above, one of the great inventions of the law is the expansion of one page into hundreds. The discourse above that merely reiterated what was already in the Table of Contents should have forewarned you to expect yet another reiteration. So here are the Conclusions.

1) **Genetic Structure.** Although nothing has been found of particular relevance, it was felt[2] that it was necessary to include a section on genetic structure because everyone would be expecting it. As pointed out above, this section will be extremely technical, requiring numerous degrees and, the fact that it represents one-sixth the cost of this book, it is absolutely essential with regard to retail price fixing.

2) **Education.** This particular area is a constant focus of attention. Years down the road, when you are a lateral transfer, you still will be asked questions such as: Were you on law review? What was your class rank? How did you do on your LSAT? You will definitely not be asked questions such as: Did you take a course on ethics? What do you think of moral constructs? What, to you, is the meaning of life?

3) **Life in a Corporation.** This has been one of those up-and-coming areas, just as there are neighborhoods that appear decrepit but sophisticated people live in them because they can't afford where they really want to live, which is any place with Travertine marble bathrooms. Years ago, in-house corporate counsel carried the stigma of being known as lackards and legal bums who just couldn't make it in the real world of private law firms. Then, with the glut of lawyers on the marketplace, corporate counsel suddenly became elevated in stature.

4) **Life in a Small Law Firm.** Sometimes relegated to the status formerly given in-house corporate counsel, small law firms are actually tiny little ova just waiting to reproduce and reproduce and reproduce until they are big law firms which then collapse into a myriad of tiny little ova that sue each other while waiting to start the replication process all over. A very small law firm is termed an intellectually stimulating place where associates get immediate

hands-on experience. A slightly larger law firm is now generally termed a "boutique." When a law firm reaches ninety attorneys, it is at the transitional stage and is termed "a firm that is about to take off." If it doesn't take off but instead stagnates or collapses, then it is the law firm that "didn't make the big push." An analogy can be made here between the above description of an expanding firm and an associate's path toward partnership, but analogies are merely a lawyer's way of adding another ten pages to a losing argument.

5) The Large Firm. A large firm has as its earmarks long hallways sometimes used for science fiction films, winding highly polished staircases (actually placed there in lieu of an in-house health club), huge libraries, computers, and beautiful secretaries who don't wear bras. There are two major differences between a large firm and a small firm: the amount of space rented, and the amount of a client's bill.

6) Clients. A client can be an individual who wants to destroy a blood relation, marry someone who might be after his money, or avoid paying income taxes. A client can also be a corporation that wants to destroy a competitor, avoid a take-over by a company that might be after its assets, or avoid paying income taxes. Within these two groups, a good client never asks questions and pays promptly. A bad client asks for an itemized bill detailing how a five minute telephone conversation about the weather has been inflated into a $20,000 fee.

7) Judges. Judges are elected or appointed to sit on a raised bench from which they can peer down the blouses of law secretaries, prospective jurors, and victims. With the usual perceptiveness of the legal process, attorneys specializing in civil law end up being criminal court judges, and attorneys with absolutely no experience on the bench are nominated to the United States Supreme Court. Judges who are kicked or fall off the bench either join firms as name partners or go on the lecture circuit. These latter are called "circuit judges."

8) Ethics. No discussion of the law would be complete without an essay on the moral structure of the law, as in payoffs and kickbacks. Of particular interest will be the analysis of the use of media, such as

A TYPICAL EXHIBIT
(THIS IS A CONTRACT, OR LEASE, OR SOMETHING)

All right, so I lied about there being no more exhibits. But I had this one hanging around from some case or other and decided to drop it in here, much in the manner of a law firm giving bulk to a matter. Clients are extremely impressed when they can barely lift a memorandum, brief or bill. Besides, the point size of this exhibit is perfect for testing one's ability to read legalese. Those with magnifying glasses, microscopes or, even better, electron microscopes, should also analyze the fine lines, between the lines, above and below the lines, and the lines themselves.

WITNESSETH that one of the curiosities of the law is that documents are always executed. People don't sign documents, they affix their signatures. If you go into a law firm and insist on signing instead of affixing, you will be told in vehement terms that signing will not lead to execution. At least it's not you who's being executed, but the document, although no one ever pauses to ask what the document did to deserve that kind of treatment.

THEREFORE is another oddity. Sometimes, it is spelled with or without the final "e." When it has the "e," a ton of words are going to come after it; without the "e," it is referring to a ton of words that came before it.

WHEREFORE seems to have been overlooked by linguistic lawyers, since it is stuck with its "e."

IN CONSIDERATION is a misplaced phrase in a contract or settlement because people executing documents have no intention of being considerate of each other. Consideration as a legal noun used to mean money, although it can now include a change in position. Just as consideration has nothing to do with being civil, a change in position does not mean crossing one's legs, sitting, standing or jumping up and down on one foot. It means a legal change in position and that generally means money.

THE PARTIES HERETO AGREE points out yet another strange twist. In the old days, and still in use in smaller firms, parties were not given Saturday nights but were instead the people affixing their signatures to execute a document. These parties had no names; they were "the party of the first part" and "the party of the second part." Additional parties had other parts assigned to them. Just to make sure that no idiot (like another attorney) might think that the executed document was binding people who had not affixed their signatures, all parties, besides having parts, had to be "parties hereto."

IN WITNESS WHEREOF was (and remains) another way of ensuring that only those affixing will be blamed for that which they have executed. Unfortunately, only the "parties hereto" are the witnesses for the affixation of most documents. Where witnesses or notaries are required for other documents, such as wills, they are culled from the staff of the law firm in which the event is taking place on the assumption that should the affixing and execution ever be attacked by someone who was not a "party hereto" and who has become upset over it, these witnesses and notaries will give a version supporting the firm which employs them.

match boxes and ads placed in buses, in bringing legal services to the poor.[3]

Exhibits

This book will not have exhibits appended to it, although exhibits are wonderful things. Take a real estate case. You can have a lease, an assignment of lease, an assignment of rents, a note, a mortgage, a deed of trust, an exchange of letters, canceled checks, plats, maps, bounds, leaps, aerial photographs, perhaps even a fragment of a brick or driveway. Each exhibit will be fifty pages long, partly typed, partly handwritten, and completely illegible. The net result is a hundred page complaint or document of sale and a thousand page appendix held together in a manner guaranteed to explosively snap open at the slightest touch.

In case you wonder where all those exhibits come from, there is a man who lives in New Jersey who has files of illegible exhibits classified by number, letter, and case. I think he is the brother-in-law of the man who supplies legal forms to all the law firms so that for fifteen cents, a law firm has something it can then have retyped, edited, retyped, added to, and so on, until that fifteen cent document has been increased overnight into a five thousand dollar document with wide enough margins to permit handwritten changes that no one will be able to decipher later on.

For those of you who desperately need the secure feeling of exhibits, sit in a chair and place the telephone directories of every major city on your lap.[4] Then begin reading this book.

Footnotes:

1. Caveat is not a talk show host but an imported Japanese car (as opposed to a non-domestic Japanese car). A "caveat emptor" has racing stripes and leather seats.
2. The "it" felt it, not me. "It's" are the literati of the law and, although impassive by nature, crop up frequently in legal documents as objective reference points.
3. "Media" is the plural of "medium" but, since it is used only in the plural, the reader might be interested in noting that the singular "media" means a soft mute and that the word "media" is drawn from Medea, the vicious witch of Greek mythology. If you find all that extremely confusing but ringing of enough background research so that you will not contest it, you are a client; if you find this footnote highly relevant and persuasive, you are on your way to making partner, if you aren't one already.
4. The efficacy of following the course detailed above is outside of the competence of the author of this treatise who specifically notes that the above should not and cannot be construed as a waiver of any claims, defenses, or causes of action the author may have on the subject from the time the world was created to the time the world blows up.

CHAPTER ONE

GENETIC STRUCTURE

Bluffing -- Childhood

If your first words were "I'll sue," you may not become a lawyer but you'll be a good client. Real lawyers choose their first words carefully, as in "If, as you state, you are my mother, prove it."

There are other early indicators. Allergic reactions to everything except blue or gray pinstriped diapers with your initials (at least three) sewn on; a physiological need for milk spiked with whiskey (particularly at the one o'clock, four o'clock and bedtime feedings); the ability to manipulate other children into paying for your breakfast, lunch, dinner, wardrobe, and prostitutes (sorry, mistresses and an illegitimate child or two) in exchange for nothing; and the ability to bluff.

Let's dwell on that last point for a moment.[1] The gene for bluffing is essential to the ribonucleic make-up of any budding lawyer. Not intelligence, because that can be bluffed. Not savvy, because that can bluffed. In fact, everything can be bluffed except one physiological occurrence, and that is only limited to male attorneys. Nowadays, though, even that can be bluffed. The budding attorney can say: "Not that, not yet, I have a fear of getting an incurable disease and since it's no good using a prophylactic," etc., etc.[2]

Thus, a child who is born to be a lawyer is born with the knack of bluffing. Bluffing means being able to sound impressive (again, not intelligent, since that's immaterial to the law), while saying absolutely nothing and knowing even less. This type of child is typically termed "precocious." For example:

11

TEACHER: Charlie, what is two times two?

CHARLIE: That is an extremely stimulating question requiring a great deal of thought and I was hoping that we could discuss this at a time more convenient for both of us.

TEACHER: Charlie, I didn't understand a word of what you were saying, although it sounded like a compliment, but, as I said, what is two times two?

CHARLIE [*with slight irritation*]: Mrs. Smith, I find that retort uncalled for. I will answer you when you have further explained exactly what it is that you would like. Time is of the essence, you know.

TEACHER: You mean, two times two equals four?

CHARLIE: Exactly. That is precisely my point.

The above example shows why bluffing is so essential to the legal mind. As will be seen later,[3] in many instances a client can solve his own problem and the lawyer can't because he doesn't know anything about the topic. The proper bluffing posture will elicit the answer from the client while making the client feel like a fool. That is extremely important for lawyer/client relationships. And that is also why having a lawyer as a client is the worst possible scenario, because no one will know the answer.

But the in-born bluffer will also recognize that where bluffing fails, a call for the troops will both solve the problem and create a large financial gain.

Suppose the teacher above had pressed Charlie for a correct answer. Charlie's recourse would have been to say:

CHARLIE: I know exactly what you are saying and I will have an

KNOWING THE LAW

Although the code of professional responsibility which establishes the high moral level of lawyers says that a lawyer should not handle a case unless he or she knows the area of law involved or can learn it without difficulty, there is no known time when a lawyer turned down a case, particularly one involving an area in which he had no knowledge. At least, no record in this universe.

In fact, a common situation is where one lawyer knows an area and another lawyer does not. The former is probably billed out to clients at one hundred dollars an hour, while the latter charges three hundred.

The knowledgeable attorney usually realizes that he will not get the other attorney's client for his own, because clients tend to live in a cloud assuming that lawyers practice the law. It is also well known that the less a lawyer knows and the more he charges, the more respected he is by clients. On the other hand, the knowledgeable attorney cannot just give the contract, settlement papers or whatever to the other attorney, since his own client will have reviewed them first and will expect to see some negotiations occur. Clients like being caught up in a sense of battle and going for the jugular; it is no fun to win right off the bat. Besides, without negotiations and redraftings, neither attorney will be able to bill the amount required for the first class, round-trip ticket to Paris or braces for the kids.

The attorney in the know will therefore coach the other attorney, suggesting to him that perhaps this clause or that wording should be changed. The other attorney will sigh and suggest that a paralegal be called in to mark up the documents while they have lunch. The attorneys will then check their watches and make the appropriate notations on their record sheets.

The above* situation is, however, not the norm. In most cases, neither attorney will have any knowledge or experience in the area requiring their utmost attention.

---

* Lawyers always refer to the "above" and "below" of documents, even though "before" and "after" would seem to be much more relevant to flat pieces of paper.

answer for you tomorrow as soon as I confer with my colleagues. This matter is too weighty for an off-the-cuff response, but requires careful consideration. Thank you.

Charlie's next step is to bluff four or five students into working overnight on the answer, even if they are capable of giving an immediate response. Better yet, if he can get them to copy mathematical proofs from various treatises, put his name on the "new" treatise and purchase a couple of illegible exhibits from our elderly gent in New Jersey (the cost to be reimbursed by the school, plus postage, handling, review time, and the outlays for an electric stapler, staples, and exhibit tabs), his presentation the following day will be quite impressive. Although Charlie himself will still have no idea about what has been solved, he will have bluffed himself into an A and a fat check.

Charlie will also use his ingrained bluffing techniques for social advantage. If he is Jewish or black, he will bluff himself into the country club. If she is a she, she will bluff the guys into believing she is a he (actually, not hard to do at that age), and the girls into believing that she is both a feminist and a homebody (the compromise here is baking cakes from mixes). If he is a WASP, he will suggest to Jews that he was circumcised, will drop a few lines in Swahili to the appropriate black and, nowadays, will hint casually to homosexuals (who invariably tend to be wealthy or have good contacts in interesting cities) that he is bi.

Another advantage of genetic bluffing is the ability to garner awards. The true lawyer-to-be will have a dozen letter sweaters by the time he graduates from high school. Later, when interviewing at law firms, he will tell the truth:[4] that the letters were for managing. To prospective clients from Jersey City, he will announce that the awards were for heroic athletics on which betting was allowed.

He will also have a dozen scholastic awards. For example, Editor-in-Chief of the school newspaper, "The Spirit." The fact that he founded "The Spirit" and put out one issue that flopped is irrelevant. He will be printed up in *Who's Who of American High*

BLUFFING A PROTEST

Here is a true story with only the facts, names, and situation changed.

While in high school, a group of students decided to protest the required salute of the flag and reading from the Bible which occurred every morning. These students thereafter refused to stand during the salute and moaned loudly during the Book of Job.

These students were threatened with suspension.

Bob, the student who had organized the protest, called the group together and gave an oration that had undoubtedly been written by a professional speechwriter from the local Democratic Club. The appropriate jokes were said prior to the segue into how the protest had to be continued regardless of personal cost or sacrifice because all of humanity, particularly the poor, underprivileged, and uneducated, were waiting with bated breath to be freed of the need to salute the flag and read the Bible, even though they were not in school and couldn't read anyway.

After the standing ovation, half the students chickened out and apologized publicly to school officials. The other half followed Bob. They were suspended the following day.

Strangely enough, Bob reappeared in school as if nothing had happened. School officials gave him a wide berth. Why? His father was friendly with a local branch of a legal organization dedicated to protecting the poor, underprivileged, uneducated, and Bob. A suit had been brought against the school, but only in Bob's name. His civil rights had been violated. The others had no civil rights unless they could afford attorneys.

Bob was thereafter accepted by one of the top colleges in the country. The others who had remained suspended were not so lucky.

Moral: Never listen to speeches.

School Students, for which honor he paid ten dollars. He will become a Merit Finalist or Scholar, and will score an average of 750 (out of 800) on his SAT's and Achievement Tests because he can bluff probability itself.

He will be class something: president, valedictorian, or chairperson of numerous committees (that he will organize himself). He will claim impressive abilities: equitation, car racing, breeding (of anything that moves), dissection (of anything that doesn't move), staying power, tolerance to alcohol and general social ailments.

He will claim to have lost his virginity at the age of nine to a stunning Swedish woman, age thirty, who still writes to him, enclosing nude photographs of herself. If he smokes cigarettes and drinks vodka by age twelve, he will be a litigator. If he brings suit against the school district, attracts national attention, and is represented by the ACLU, he will become a politician, a professor of constitutional law, or a social advocate. If he successfully sponsors a wet T-shirt contest, he will become a corporate partner in a major firm.

Learning Not To Communicate

The only strain on his bluffing talents will occur in English classes and, later, English as a Second Language classes. The budding lawyer is naturally incapable of writing a clear short story, or a precise, erudite essay. His first attempt at writing will be as follows:

WHAT I DID THIS SUMMER™

by CHARLIE

What I did this summer is of no concern to anyone and if you attempt to pursue your inquiries in any manner, method or form, I can assure you that paper shall be met with paper and motion with motion, until this frivolous invasion of my privacy is promptly terminated. This essay is not meant, intended or to be construed as a waiver or

16

release of any and all claims, defenses, or causes of action I may or may not have.

Thank you.

Charles

The first attempt at a short story will be just as moving:

A SHORT™ STORY™

THE ANSWER™

BY BUFFY, JR.™

Timothy O'Mara (hereinafter "Tim") and Mary O'Timothy (hereinafter "Mary" or "Babs") met in or about June, 198_ (the "Meeting") at the corner of Fourth and Main (the "Meeting Place"). Their initial intentions were unclear. However, it soon became indisputable that Tim's intentions were, to say the lease [*sic*], salacious. In any event, Mary forthright and without equivocation stated as her answer: "NO."

It cannot be gainsaid that NO is an explicit expression of denial.

17

Thank you.

Buffy, Jr.

The first history essay will reveal a genetic pattern essential for any successful lawyer. It will not be duplicated here, since writing as a lawyer will be covered in a later chapter of this book. The sum and substance of it is that the essay will contain two double-spaced sentences on each page of a ten page paper, and five hundred footnotes. Once this technique of writing is discovered by the budding attorney, it will be transferred to short stories, poems, and letters home from Europe.

Beyond Bluffing

Beyond bluffing,[5] the born lawyer will attract money because of his mere presence. And it won't be because he looks poor, starved, or in need of money -- just the reverse, it will be because he looks like someone who deserves to have your money. Grandparents will tousle his hair and give him five dollars on the spot. Neighbors will give him dollar bills for UNICEF on Halloween night, even though he does not represent UNICEF. His allowance will be increased weekly -- well above the COLA index -- and he will receive year-end bonuses.

This child will be no innocent, either. He will not blush when he bluffs or receives money or creates accolades for himself. He will never lose sleep over anything, even if he is a bed wetter. Bed wetting

18

is someone else's concern, such as the person who has to clean up after him. Note: all chronic bed wetting means is that the child will probably not become a litigator. Litigators are born with extremely large bladders so that they can spend an entire day berating witnesses and not have to worry about going to the bathroom. Besides, bathrooms in most courthouses are either inaccessible or closed for repairs. In criminal court, lawyers who are stupid enough to go to the public bathroom deserve what they get.

These children will also be born with a silver credo in their mouths: Don't trust anyone; get everyone to trust you; and screw them when the time is right.

One scenario is this: Charlie befriends Dougie because Dougie's father is city councilman. Charlie (age 8) always arrives at Dougie's house just as cocktail hour is beginning and sips his Shirley Temple while nodding graciously at every word Dougie's father says, even if Dougie's father is on his third martini and is saying, "Thish life shuckles."

Charlie, however, does something punishable at school and forgets to wear gloves when he does it: steals pencils, drills a hole into the girls' shower room, leaves dog shit in a paper bag on a teacher's chair. Assuming no other victims are available, Charlie's decision is whether to turn in Dougie as the culprit and lose cocktail hour and a powerful contact, but thereby maintain his own clean record and build up brownie points with the administration of the school; or, turn himself in before he is pounced upon, in the hope of salvaging the situation by proving his mettle and analogizing his actions to George Washington and the cherry tree.

But the in-born lawyer is genetically incapable of ever admitting that he has done something wrong or even a tinge unethical, and a comparison to George Washington in this day and age is of no political value. So Charlie now has two alternatives: turn in Dougie outright and befriend Buffy, whose father would like to be councilman -- Charlie will supply[6] Buffy's father with the notebooks he has been keeping of Dougie's father's statements made during cocktail hour and will then become the youngest campaign manager in the history of American politics; or, turn in Dougie through the use of innuendo and rumor, thereby keeping Dougie's friendship, the friendship of his father, and allowing himself additional time to assess the possible outcome of the upcoming election. At this tender stage of his life, Charlie will select the latter alternative.

Summer Camp

The genetic lawyer-to-be will have a heyday at summer camps. He will attend camps with names like The Camp of Lords, Camp Or-A-Tori, Camp Suda-Bastard, and Camp Stabin-Back. These camps have brochures that list a distinguished board of directors down the lefthand margin. Instead of sending his clothes in trunks or duffle bags, the lad will have them shipped in leather suitcases that have his initials on them in gold. He will wear the camp colors (in pinstripe) but, for some reason, they will look better on him than on the other campers. Even after a hard day of riding English-style, his hair will fall naturally into place.

He will also test his wings with regard to politicking himself to the top among a group of people he has never before met. Although the last one onto the camp bus, Charlie will somehow manage to have the best seat, next to the camp director. By the time the bus arrives at the camp, he will have a written agreement from the director granting him special rights, such as fresh fruit once a day, his own horse, and unlimited passes for going to town.

Although the last one into the bunkhouse, Charlie will somehow get the best bunk, situated next to the counselor, whom he will graciously charm to the point where Charlie will never have to take a turn at cleaning the urinals. Two nerdy children will immediately latch onto Charlie and, in their blind idolatry, will insist on buying him candy at the canteen and making his bed, even if he wets it.

Although he is a terrible actor, Charlie will negotiate the starring role (whether male or female) in the camp's play.

Halfway through the summer, Charlie will have spread rumors that have everyone convinced that he has had sex with all the attractive female counselors (even if they are in their early twenties and he is nine).

During the color war, Charlie will leap off the lake platform before his team has touched base but will not be penalized.

Charlie also will have come to camp with a stack of postcards already filled out and consisting of numerous footnotes about what a wonderful time he is having, although it all takes a great deal of effort, and could he have large sums of money sent posthaste?

For her part, Buffy will be the only nine year old with a training bra. Rumors will be spread that she has turned down offers of affairs made by most of the male counselors, but that she has also given of herself to one or two counselors. One of those counselors will be extremely ugly but from a powerful family.

Buffy will, at times, permit Ginny and Marie to apply makeup to her face and brush her hair, and she will be the only girl to have English riding boots, jodphurs, a white silk blouse, a black velvet riding helmet, and a well-used crop. She will ride both side-saddle and in the saddle, and use her crop with alacrity and charm. When she smiles, she will dimple in her left cheek, but when she is extremely pleased with something or someone, a dimple will appear in her right cheek.

She never passes gas or burps like the other girls her age when they are playing around and she knows everything under the sun about periods. Her ears were pierced when she was two and she is the only camper to wear diamond stud earrings to the Red Cross swimming test. Her best stroke is the sidestroke although, for a lark (or any potential client), she will do the breast stroke.

For the camp play, not only does she get the best role (male or female), but she will rewrite the play to give herself the best role. She will be placed in charge of makeup and scenery, while Charlie takes care of printing up the Playbill that he will sell to the parents the night of the play.

Towards the end of the camp season, Buffy and Charlie will be in outright competition with each other. Each will spread rumors about the other that are unprintable, yet they will maintain amiable, friendly relations. This situation will utterly confuse everyone else at the camp since, on the one hand, it appears that Charlie and Buffy

IT'S ALL MERIT, NOT CONTACTS AT ALL

Without spilling the beans on how one can definitely become a partner in a major law firm, following is a typical wedding announcement that might be found in a major newspaper.

JONEMAN TO MARRY DRUCKMANN, LAWYER

Mary Joneman was married to George Druckmann at Our Lady of the Plaintiffs' Church today by the Very Reverend Irving Leff, *SPC, RN, AD, RFM*. The bride was attended by her sister, Alice. The best man for the bridegroom was Steven Justice, the third husband of the bridegroom's fourth ex-wife. This was the first marriage for the bride after two long-term affairs.

The bride graduated *cum laude* from Bryn Mawr College and received her masters from the Smithtown School of Design. She works as assistant vice president in her father's company, Wishworks, a design and manufacturing firm.

The bridegroom received his bachelors of arts from Rutgers and his law degree from California State Institute. He is a partner in the law firm of Mudge, Roth, Fish, Bein, Lebowitz, Druckmann and O'Hara. His father, Harold Druckmann, was a founding partner in the firm, the largest in the country.

are lovers and, on the other hand, that Charlie and Buffy hate each other.

On the last day of camp, Charlie and Buffy will exchange addresses but will not keep in touch unless one or the other becomes engaged years later and is written up in a quality newspaper. If it is Buffy,·Charlie will send her Baccarat crystal as a gift. If it is Charlie, Buffy will send a casual note sealed in an envelope lined with gold foil.

Family Crises

The genetic lawyer-to-be also exhibits himself during family crises. By the time he is five, he will have surreptitiously rooted through the private documents of his parents and will know who is powerful in the family and who is not. The seating arrangements at Thanksgiving and Christmas meals will be extremely important to him. He, being knowledgeable of wines, will serve, beginning with the powerful family members and giving the dregs, cork bits and all, to the weaker members.

If the head of the family is a ninety year old man who has had six strokes and who sits in a wheelchair and slobbers, it will be Charlie who is by his side hour after hour, whispering and nodding as if the old man, who has been incapable of speaking for fifteen years, is giving him lessons in life. When the old man finally dies, Charlie either will be the sole heir or will "discover" a recently dated will naming him heir.

When Charlie is old enough to drive, he will accept the hand-me-down used family car with equanimity and then sell it on the open market for more than it originally retailed for. Then he will go to a new car dealer and negotiate a price well below retail for what is on hand. With the remaining money, he will begin investing in the stock market, sometimes cutting school to sit in his broker's office and watch the tape.

Charlie will eventually have a margin account. Other family members, at first with a laugh, thinking how cute he is, will give him their portfolios to manage. For those family members who are powerful, Charlie will increase the value of their portfolios tenfold. For the rest, he will maintain their portfolios at original value, although only he will recognize that that means an actual loss because of inflation, and he will charge them a ten percent commission for his advice.

But Charlie's real dream is to have enough money to begin purchasing real estate. His goal is to start with a condominium where the down payment is only ten percent. He will then rent that out and take out a second mortgage to finance the down payment on another home that he will rent out. If any of his lessees should default on their rental payments, Charlie will have no qualms about having them evicted according to the letter of the law,[7] even if it is the middle of winter and the lessee's wife and kids are deathly ill.

Charlie will innately recognize that a successful person separates issues such as "letter of the law" from irrelevancies such as "humanitarian concerns." Thus, if he ends up holding the mortgage and note on his parents' home and they default on the note, he will have them summarily tossed out while muttering what a shame it is that debtors' prison was abolished in this country.

College

From birth on, the genetic lawyer-to-be will have only one goal: to finish high school, finish college, finish law school, and become a partner at a major firm. He will not pause for breath in that pursuit and will look incredulously at any lawyer who took time off between any of those pursuits to do something stupid, such as spending a year in Italy studying art, or living in New Mexico working as a janitor and writing the great American novel.

In college -- and more likely than not, it will be an Ivy League school -- the budding lawyer will major in political science while dabbling in economics. If possible, he will get out of any required courses he considers non-essential, such as Composition. If he is forced to learn a foreign language, it will be Japanese. He will

ON THE LSATs

There is no surviving member of the team which first thought up the LSATs, so we no longer know exactly what the acronym stands for. What is known is that anyone who wants to go to law school has to take the test at least once. It is also known that the most important part of the test is getting together the money to pay for it. The next most important part is getting together the money to pay for having "verified" copies of the score sent to law schools.

The test consists of one question divided into six thousand four hundred sub-parts, heavily footnoted. Fluency in English is not only not required, but is usually considered a detriment. In the short answer part, choices are limited to True, False, and Bill. The part on ethics (contained in a footnote) is answered with Right, Wrong, or Bill.

Some recent examples of essay questions are these:

1. You are in your firm at nine o'clock on a Tuesday night. Should you go home and, if so, why and how?

2. Your client does not remember the events leading up to the lawsuit even though he is the plaintiff. Explain to him the difference between memory and legal facts.

3. You marry the daughter of a name partner and the dowry consists of your being hired as an associate and being given your own office. Discuss the upside and downside of: a) remaining married; b) remaining married and having affairs; c) filing joint returns; d) vacationing together at Club Med.

As pointed out in other chapters, your LSAT score will often be a primary topic of conversation whether you are applying to law school, your first law job, or your tenth lateral transfer. Frequently, firms will insist that you pay to have "verified" scores sent over. At that stage of your career, their lack of belief in your honesty is yet another indication of how much credence lawyers put in their own code of ethics. (Either that, or the firms receive a commission on each "verified" score sent to them.)

25

concentrate fervently on learning racquet ball, tennis, golf, and touch football.

The budding lawyer will learn that the easiest way to get a good grade with the least amount of work is to plagiarize. One often reads articles about the straight A student (whether at college or law school) who is caught plagiarizing, but now you don't have to wonder why they do it. They are playing the law game. Unfortunately, they are playing it a few years too early. Later, they will not only get away with the game, but also will be paid handsomely for the effort.

In contrast, the lawyer-not-to-be will struggle for each grade. After all, he began life wearing disposable diapers over a horrendous rash that did not disappear until he turned twelve. He trembled on his first date and carries around the memory of his first sexual conquest as something to cherish rather than brag about. When he received a letter in track, it was for breaking the school record in the 400. He never had a first car, but instead had three newspaper routes.

Our lawyer-not-to-be is still an innocent who believes that friends are friends and that morality, whether social or religious, has a significance in life that is important to fulfillment and well-being. He cares for every member of his family and, when the dog needs to go out, he stops whatever he is doing so that the animal will not suffer.

If he does not cry openly during the screening of certain films, he feels the same emotional upheaval as when he reads of people being tortured.

When the lawyer-to-be, looking worried, approaches him and says that he is in big trouble unless he gets help finishing an essay on a topic no one else has written on, he cheerfully helps his friend. When that same friend later spreads vicious rumors about him, the lawyer-not-to-be merely shakes his head and believes that no one would be stupid enough to listen to those rumors. Even when he is brought up before a college board to be examined on charges stemming from those innuendos, the lawyer-not-to-be will not disparage the name of his former friend.

At that point in life, the successful lawyer-not-to-be will be expelled from school and become a bicycle repairman, living happily ever after with his wife and child in a small house needing a coat of paint.

The budding lawyer, however, will expand his influence on campus, being seen at the right parties with the right people. If he is not the editor of the school newspaper, he will have an affair with one of its journalists, ensuring that his name appears frequently in front page columns. Those blurbs will say things like, "Charlie has again succeeded in bringing yet another important personage to campus, this time Senator X who, after lunching with Charlie, will discuss the role of government in the legal process with the members of the ..."; "Remember So-and-so, the famous actress who came to our school as a freshman last year? Of late, she has been seen visiting with Dean Y, attended to by Charlie ..."; and "The Secret Society of Most Successful People, the prestigious on-campus group composed of outstanding alumni in politics, business and the law, has announced that Charlie will become its newest member ..."

If the law were like sports, Charlie would be the number one pick in the fall draft. As it is, he will whiz through his LSAT exam using his heightened bluffing techniques and will be accepted at all the ranked law schools. Assuming student loans are still being given, Charlie will then face two crucial tests: Is the interest rate on the student loan low enough so that if he invests the loan in a relatively secure market, he will end up making a good return? And, if the tax code does not permit a deduction for the interest on the loan, can he hide it as a business expense?

What You Aren't Supposed To Know ...

Footnotes:

1. Dwelling on a last point is a nut and bolt of the law even though it may sound, to a layman, illogical that one should dwell on a previous point when all the dwelling is yet to come in the technical dwelling dissertation. Dwelling on last points has two beneficial results: 1) it keeps clients from dwelling on the size of their bill; and 2) it makes judicial clerks believe that something important has been stated.
2. "Prophylactic" is not a medical term, but a legal term, as in "prophylactic measures." The use of the phrase occurs in the following context: Lawyers loudly discuss prophylactic measures in crowded elevators.
3. In the law, things will be "seen" or "clarified" or "made clear" later. "Later" is a Latin word meaning "there is no answer or solution to this question but if you keep reading you may fall asleep." "Clarified" has an additional meaning, to wit: the skimming of fat from melted butter to leave behind ghee, which is applied to the palms prior to shaking hands with a client.
4. In the law, telling the truth is normally synonymous with "slip of the tongue." The instance cited above is the only exception to the general rule found by this author after extensive research.
5. "Beyond Bluffing" was not the film that was the subject matter of United States v. Four Hundred Reels, ### U.S. ### (19__), a case that had the famous quote: "I know it when I feel it." "Beyond bluffing" is a term employed in white collar crime, as where the defendant really does give the prosecutor cement shoes.
6. "Supply" is a Latin term loosely translated as "I will give this to you as a favor and you will pay me for the favor on my terms." Supply-side economics, for example, means that the government will provide services to the people and the people will supply money to the government upon demand.
7. "Letter of the law" is a euphemism that is sometimes symbolized as a dead fish wrapped in newspaper. Whether or not you eat the fish, you will still be billed for it.

CHAPTER TWO

LAW SCHOOL

Professors And Sex

Most law school professors have never practiced law but nonetheless have a healthy appetite for young girls. To digress[1] for a moment, it is easy to spot a salacious prof. If you are in a class where the professor opens the session with the comment, "I didn't get to shave this morning because she kept me up all night and then I couldn't find my razor blade," he is suggesting that he had an affair the night before (and would, therefore, like another one that night), or that he is losing his memory, or that he is drunk at ten in the morning.[2] If he compounds such statements with an exhibition of memory that only recollects the names of the nubile young female students with their chests squeezed into tight cashmere sweaters and their firm thighs pressed into designer jeans, then you are on to something. Some circumstantial evidence: he continues to call on those girls even though they know absolutely nothing about the subject matter at hand. Note: if one or more of them get top grades, you have reached the level of a rebuttable inference. Double note: if one of them also gets the Am. Jur. award, she might be worth dating.

Other examples abound.[3] You trudge up five filthy flights of metal stairs for a meeting with the professor and his door is closed. You knock. What had sounded like the heavy breathing of a faulty air conditioning unit suddenly ceases, replaced by sounds of belt buckles scraping across a wood floor, shoes being dragged from beneath couches, and zippers being zipped. If, after a three minute wait, the door opens and the professor is standing there with a nervous smile on his face and you can see a former Am. Jur. winner squatting on the floor looking over xeroxed cases and the professor says, "Oh. Did we have an appointment this afternoon?" -- you have just experienced another example involving the evolution of law as social policy.

Outright admissions do occur, as where the professor and the student are openly living together, holding hands, and smooching in the hallways. As a law student, though, you should accept that display of affection with a few grains of salt. More likely than not, the prof is married to the Dom. Rel.[4] prof and has decided to begin living the good life while she tries to figure out how to draft a separation agreement and a proposed judgment of divorce. He knows that if he waits for her to gain practical experience, he could well end up impotent from old age before she even calculates the court's filing fee.

By the way, those professors who interview students with their doors open and their secretaries directly outside have probably practiced law and had one disciplinary proceeding brought against them.

Courses

As previously noted, most professors have never practiced law, which may explain why law school courses are completely dissociated from law. Take contracts (actually, you have no choice). You begin with a series of cases dating back four centuries. Do you think you are ever going to appear before a bewigged justice sitting on the King's or Queen's Bench? There's been a lot of change in areas such as third party beneficiary law, but the relevance of a case dated 1510 and where f's replace s's was always beyond me. Are you ever shown a real contract? No? Ask the prof for a copy of his employment contract if he's on a year-to-year basis. If he doesn't have a contract, ask him about the employment-at-will doctrine, prevalent in most states and permitting an employer to fire an employee at will (which, oddly enough, is why it's called "employment-at-will" instead of something else).

Real estate is the same. There, you can at least read your own lease, but will you have any idea as to what to do at a closing? Will you learn anything about the assignment of rents? No. Instead, you will learn what enfeoff means. It is a touching word, listed as archaic in every dictionary. Somehow, I have yet to hear it come up in general conversation with a client. "Are you enfeoffed, sir?" Don't be surprised if the client slaps your face.

The course I remember with the greatest fondness, since my first law firm job involved a litigation position, is Civil Procedure. It was a two semester course and the first semester was spent analyzing Pennoyer v. Neff, a Supreme Court decision that has no precedential value. The second semester was spent analyzing Schaffer v. Heitner and long arm jurisdiction in a quasi-in-rem context that also has little life left to it and will therefore arise only in extreme situations. Matters considered irrelevant were time periods for filing; what should be filed; manner of service; motion practice. Little things like that.

A related course, Evidence, was also dramatically surreal. My professor used to draw what only could have been breasts on the board and then mark them up with probability levels. A colleague of mine, during his first trial, put his learning to use by drawing breasts on a blackboard facing the jury. He was called to the bench, where the judge leaned over and whispered: "What the fuck do you think you're doing?"

My friend erased the breasts and summed up as follows: "Gentlemen and ladies of the jury, in this case we are concerned with the preponderance of the evidence. Not clear and convincing evidence. Not proof beyond a reasonable doubt. To put that into clearer terms, you need, philosophically, to find by a weight factor of fifty-one percent that I have proved what needed to be proved. Not seventy-five percent. Not ninety-one and a half percent. Just fifty-one percent."

In real life, winning by the preponderance of the evidence in front of, for example, New York City jurors, means slowly pushing down the aisle the wheelchair on which reclines your tormented client. Your client's hair will be an utter mess, since you will have cut it yourself prior to trial and added streaks of gray (even if your client is a teenager). His suit will be utterly decrepit, although clean. His shirt will be white. His tie will be conservative gray. One sock will have a hole in it above the ankle. One shoe will be missing a heel. The wife, sitting in the gallery, will sob loudly and hysterically at appropriate moments, especially when loss of consortium is being tried. That's preponderance of the evidence. It's also a nice, fat contingency fee.

If playing the percentages of sufficient evidence can only be taught by drawing breasts, imagine the difficulty professors have in getting across the concept of hearsay. Hearsay is usually thought of as evidence consisting of what someone told someone else who is now sweating violently on the witness stand. Hearsay is not admissible. "And what did so-and-so say to you?" "Objection!" That is, hearsay is usually not admissible. Because hearsay is sometimes admissible. There are exceptions. Exceptions are called things like "prior consistent statements" by the person on the stand or "admissions" made by a party not on the stand. A prior consistent statement, of course, can either be consistent or inconsistent, just as an admission made by a party not on the stand can be a statement not made by that party but by someone else somehow speaking for that party. Similarly, if the person who made the statement is available to take the stand, his statements can be repeated by the person on the stand if the statments gave a present sense impression, or were an excited utterance, or expressed a mental condition. On the other hand, if the person who said those things is not available to testify, then one is stuck with exceptions like dying statements and former testimony. But on the other hand, the statement may not be offered as hearsay, because hearsay testimony is offered to prove the truth of the matter; one could argue that the statement is being presented not for its truth but just as a statement. Then again, there might be hearsay included within hearsay, but that's all right, too, if each hearsay within the hearsay and the hearsay itself are subject to an exception or not presented for the truth of the matter.

I won't say what the professor drew on the board to explain hearsay. Why is hearsay such an overly complicated topic? *Because it is the only legal term not derived from Latin!* It is the Old English form for "heard say," as in, "I know nothing except what I heard say." If it could be changed to something like dicere-audivi, a lot of these hearsay problems (including how to teach it as an anatomical principle) would disappear.

Legal Research And Writing

Another required and utterly useless course is Writing, or Legal Drafting, or English as a Second Language. This course teaches you how to research and draft a memorandum of law. Let's overlook research for now since in the real practice of law, research means one year of sitting in the library picking your ass and the rest of your legal life living off that one year's worth of research.

Unlike professors of substantive law, such as contracts or torts, professors of legal research and writing tend to have practiced law prior to teaching. These professors are inevitably hired for one year terms at extremely low pay. Their hope is to teach research and writing for one or two years, then move up to the substantive realm, where salaries (at the top schools) are not at all bad.

Why lawyers who used to work at law firms end up in the lowest paying teaching positions handing out assignments culled from back issues of MAD Magazine is one of the deep mysteries of life. They say it is because they decided to dedicate their lives to molding future legal minds.

Some people say it is because these "assistant" professors could not hack legal research and writing at a law firm. But if that is so, it means they are not genetic lawyers. Assuming the truth of that proposition, one would have to say that therefore they are incapable of teaching the legal research and writing necessary for bluffing one's way through a law firm. Thankfully, these teachers are so winded from their brief association with law firms that they emulate absurdity with the best of them.

The practice memorandum of law is meant to test the mettle of the grammatical student. The genetically inclined law student will suddenly find himself not needing to bluff writing anymore, since his

ON THE LAWFUL PRONUNCIATION OF LATIN

Latin word	Legal pronunciation
a confectione	cookie
a fortiori	afersherorororeeee
a manu servus	maid
a posteriori	aposhterorooroeee
ab actis	abacus
acquietandis plegiis	stand plegies
ad interim	ahem
ad rectum	(won't be said because of uncertainty as to meaning)
advocati fisci	avocados fish, eh?
animo et corpore	enema corpse
causa causans	Cousin, Cousine
cause sine qua non	cauzah sine key nuhn
caveat emptor	hey, you hired me
corpus juris	corpse juries
damnum absque injuria	dabnab injury, ah
filius	feelus
in haec verba	in heek werb
jus accrescendi	juice a crescent
lex loci delictus	lex losee delicious
licet	like it
lite pendente	light a pendant
nolo contendere	Watergate
non compos mentis	everyone else
particeps criminis	party keps crime in iss
per rationes	per rasheeuns
prima facie	primmah fayshee
quare obstruxit	queer obstructs it
subpoena duces tecum	sub peena dooshies take em

ready recourse to stunted language and lengthy footnotes will stand him in good stead.

What about the former English major? Needless to say, an acquaintance with English as a first language proves right off the bat that the student has no intention of succeeding as a lawyer. Lawyers-to-be major in subjects like political science or economics. The person who will succeed in legal writing is the person capable of drafting a redundant, imprecise memo littered with citations that precisely imitate the "blue book." The blue book is a costly little blue book which dictates how a cite to a case or statute is to be written regardless of whether the cite is morally accurate. This book is published by one of the leading universities that can always use an extra dime; purchasing revised editions on an annual basis, even though there is never anything revised, is a ritual no law student or lawyer can escape, although the book itself will never be referred to except in a legal writing course.

Was Socrates A Lawyer?

Professors rely on a method of teaching called Socratic, presumably because Socrates grilled his students in like manner and came up with Plato. Plato, however, did not become a lawyer, but a philosopher, and he would have failed miserably if he had been thrust into the limelight of Part I, New York Supreme.

Another unusual aspect of selecting Socrates as a monicker of the law is that he was Greek, not Roman, and our legal system is not only derived from the Roman system, but one of the true pleasures for a lawyer is to completely mispronounce Latin legalese. Besides, the fellow couldn't even argue himself out of a death sentence.

In truth, the primary reason for using the Socratic method is to ensure that students never enjoy eating for at least one year, since law school classes are arranged to take place either directly after or before a meal.

The Socratic method as used in law schools abstractly translates into a medium of quiz and answer that is supposed to stretch young minds so that enough space will exist between the ears to memorize useless facts and archaic concepts of law. A horror film released a few years ago showing the heads of people expanding to the point of bloody explosions was actually shot during a law school class and showed the reactions of those students who were not going to succeed as lawyers anyway.

The Socratic method ensures that students realize that truth has no solid foundation and probably does not exist. Of the six thousand two hundred questions asked during law school, three thousand have their premises changed mid-argument by the professor.

The best questions occur in Criminal Law. For example: "If X goes to the top of a six story building intending to leap off and end his life and does leap off; and Y, sitting in his office on the fourth floor of the building, intending to kill X later that day, is loading the pistol he purchased for the purpose; and Y sees X passing by on his way to the sidewalk; and Y shoots X in a physical area such that X doubtlessly would have died but for the fact that the sidewalk killed him first; did Y murder X in the first degree?"

Another good one: "If A, B, and C are stranded on a boat in the middle of the ocean and have run out of food; and A intends to eat C; and A does and B does not protest or attempt to prevent A from doing so; is B guilty of aiding and abetting in the death of C?"

As one begins to stutter through an answer, a professor will shift the hypothetical by adding facts or, more likely, claiming that the facts were always, indeed, as they now stand. In the latter hypothetical, B nibbled on one of C's fingers after the fact, or took a surreptitious sip of blood.

Of course, all Criminal Law hypotheticals can be changed to provide for general rape and mayhem. X, bleeding to death on the sidewalk, is viciously buggered by A, who survived the boat ride. Is it buggery if X is alive but unconscious? If X is dead?[5]

Torts is an area of the law permitting endless variations on hypotheticals since, whereas a mass murderer kills at most a hundred people before tiring out, torts dwells on those chain reactions that can wipe out an entire world. "If A brings his car into the repair shop to be repaired by B; and B repairs the car; and A drives the car onto the freeway; and A's car crashes into C's car which crashes into D's car, where D is drunk, and D's car crashes into E's car, and E's car crashes into F's car which does not have working headlights in violation of state statute, and F's car crashes into G's trailer that is violating state law because it has too many tires and the trailer crashes into H's car, killing H and maiming H's daughter who takes ballet in school, and ..."

Why add on matters such as the repair of A's car? So that the hypothetical can be changed just as a student nears a conclusion. B did repair the car. B did not repair the car and did or did not tell A of that fact. B believed he repaired the car but the parts he used were defective. B was not a repairmen but a numbers' runner and A did or did not know that and did or did not place an illegal bet, and then B raped A in the back room just for the heck of it.

After a thousand such shifts, I developed a manner of answering variable hypotheticals that is guaranteed to succeed once with each professor. This is the technique of answering with a rambling yet firm discourse on your childhood. The drawback is that you are revealing a part of yourself to those genetic lawyers-to-be who tape record everything for use against you later on. It is therefore suggested that, if you use the technique, you expound on someone else's childhood.

Another technique which has been applied with some success is to answer a hypothetical using your own fact pattern and insisting that that is exactly what the professor has stated the question to be. Since professors can barely follow their own facts and issues, they will not take a chance on having the entire class hooting them down and will permit you to continue. If you succeed here, you can always add more insult to the injury by changing your fact pattern mid-stream. If you get away with this technique, you are well on your way to becoming a professor.

The third reason for Socratic questioning is that professors don't have to prepare for class. Professors know, for example, that out of a class of fifty students, there will be three in-bred lawyers-to-be[6] who will dominate the class with idiotic statements. The professor will therefore call on the nervous wreck who always sits in the last row and who will proceed to answer in a high-pitched quavering voice. The in-bred students will then mercilessly attack the answer for the remainder of the class. I have personally observed professors and in-breds driving a wreck (who, to the rest of us, might be termed a human being) to: vomit; cry; faint; urinate on the spot; faint; have a nervous breakdown.

In the event the in-breds are all out sick, and the professor has forgotten his hypotheticals (probably because the woman the night before hid them along with his razor), the professor can fall back on simplistic Socracy. "Charlie, what is the case name? Which court? What year? Name the plaintiff and the defendant. What is the issue being analyzed? What are the facts? What is the conclusion of law?"

Law Review

So far, it has been shown that professors like sex; first year law school classes are a waste of time; and the Socratic method works well only if you wear a toga and live in the West Village. What are the students themselves doing during that first year? Those students who begin law school married are getting divorced. Everyone is cruising everyone else, including professors. The genetic lawyers-to-be have already gotten jobs as research assistants to certain professors. Black students are clinging together as if there is a lynch mob around every corner. Male Hasidic students are moaning in the lounge.[7] And everyone is gung-ho on law review and moot court, with the emphasis on the former.

Since *everyone* is asked whether he or she was on law review, it can be seen that law review is extremely important as a career move. It is a way of distinguishing students, although not in terms of legal ability. In fact, law firms have to teach law review associates how not to write law review articles. Nor is law review a benchmark of learning. Most law review students only get the chance to do endless cite checking on weekends and law review editors only learn how to become abrupt and to expect other people to do the work for them.

What is the actual value of law reviews? They contain two types of articles: those by professors vehemently arguing some personal

FEMALE LAW INTERNS

There are so many stories (and some photographs) concerning female law students interning at firms of varying sizes and prestige that it's a pity you don't have them. Here are some synopses:

The first day of work, she is asked to water plants, bring coffee, shepardize and give manicures. [Note: shepardizing means checking rows of numbers to see if a case is still good and where it has been cited in other cases.]

Two females are hired at small firm. Three days later, the one wearing see-through blouses and slit skirts is given a raise; the other is fired.

A woman soon discovers that a wedding band has absolutely no value in a law firm except to twist it around the finger to work off a case of nerves.

A female working for a sole practitioner is never asked to his office (which is probably a telephone booth) but, after doing research at her school's library, must drop off her findings at his apartment nights and weekends where she gets to exercise by running around his dining room table.

Very common at large firms: The intern is told by the male senior partner who is on the hiring committee that it would behoove her to have an affair with him even though he is married and has three children (all boys) in law school.

Used to be very common until newspapers started to pick up on it: Female interns at large firms told to participate in wet T-shirt contests.

Female interns at summer suppers must dance every slow dance with short, groping, senior partners.

The encroaching sense of doom as the female intern realizes that among all the female interns, she will not given an offer to return because she refused to have the nose job on moral grounds.

belief in an "objective" manner that includes misciting or misquoting cases; and those by students, whose articles appear as NOTES, arguing some personal belief in an "objective" manner that includes misciting or misquoting cases. But since every law school puts out a law review, and they are periodical, the odds are increased that a law firm can find a law review article vehemently arguing an otherwise untenable position, which article will then be cited throughout a brief as if it were God's word.

While being on law review may be construed by firms as a desired ability to bluff or be politic, many genetic lawyers-to-be get on via the cite-checking couch (with a law review editor), or through wining, dining, and bedding the legal writing instructor who is an "advisor" to the board of editors.

Moot Court

I cannot say much about moot court because it was always a moot question for me. I never saw much sense in arguing about still more hypotheticals in front of "real" judges. I have, however, heard of some judges getting somewhat drunk at the receptions held after competitions and making passes at certain contestants. But more on drunk judges later.

Mootness is an actual legal term meaning that a matter will not be heard by a court because the issue has been resolved on its own, typically outside of the legal process (as where a pregnant woman sues on her pregnancy and gives birth before the issue can be heard). Law school moot court for some reason uses the word even though the hypotheticals are not moot, but really strange. Often, mythical lands are created and populated with mythical laws which have a complex and mysterious impact on the mythical populace. Thankfully, the populace is always given enough money to see a lawsuit through the appellate process, something which is not always true in our own reality. But maybe they don't have to pay all that much, since their lawyers are only students.

Moot court does serve one major purpose. There are state-wide, regional, and national moot court competitions. Moot court competitions are the football tournaments law schools wish they had. Instead of going over plays on the blackboard, the coach drills his team in oration, debate, and building to the kill. Instead of wearing pads, tights, and sneakers, the students wear three-piece suits and Rolex watches. But there are referees (the judges), and there is a cheerleading section (the audience) -- and the winners get trophies that go in glass cases.

Drinking

Law students are also introduced to the most important class they will ever take in law school: Drinking I. No doubt about it, lawyers can pack it away, and the fool who can't hold his or her own better forget the whole deal. Law schools are built in neighborhoods zoned for bars. Not real bars, where a man can go in, drink Muscatel, and knife someone in the back (and then rape and bugger the corpse). But fake bars, with beautiful fake wood, and beautiful fake wood carvings, and beautiful fake music, and beautiful waitresses and waiters, and a bartender who has a Ph.D. in sociology.

The true budding lawyer needs no introduction to drinking. He had his liver removed when he was ten. The others, however, must undergo the proper tutelage. For example, many senior litigators and corporate attorneys drink Chivas Regal, although the more ambitious will drink unblended scotch, such as Glenlivet. Some litigators and bankruptcy attorneys sip Stoli, Absolut, or Finlandia on the rocks with a twist. Tort lawyers who work on a contingency fee basis[8] drink Jim Beam or Gordon's during the trial, and the good stuff if they win. Only legal services and union-side labor lawyers will be obnoxious enough to order a no-name liquor mixed with tonic or soda.

Drinking I further provides that in the event a lawyer has to vomit, he will do so in a manner which is unobtrusive and does not mess up his clothes. This is extremely important during long meetings.

What You Aren't Supposed To Know ...

The law student who can drink ten drinks and not have to go to the bathroom will be a litigator.

The female law student who drinks ten drinks, loses her virginity, and doesn't even fake an orgasm will not succeed as a lawyer but will make a good legal secretary.

Sexual Analyses

First year law students will also learn the true meaning of sex: talk about it, ogle everything that moves, and be terrible in bed. Time is of the essence in the law. Trying to please your bedmate, unless he or she is a paying client, is a waste of time. Besides, after a day of Socratic questioning and being fondled by professors, who really cares about true love and good sex?

Sexual *predicaments* will be prevalent, in large part because law students are not given the leeway to mature as human beings. These problems are then analyzed amidst groups of students as if they were the facts and issues of a case. Some of the patterns can become quite complex, as where a male student is bedding both a law review editor and an older, married female student who feels she has outgrown her husband, while he is really in love with a waitress who has no future. In a way, analyzing these rapid mix-and-match relationships to the death is good training for life at a law firm. First, *emotional* involvements with purported lovers are frowned upon.

Second, now that permanent, transmittable sexual diseases are in the popular mind, the analyses are perfect training for formulating lawsuits putting economic values on issues such as getting herpes.

Third, most states have adopted equitable distribution laws and some (such as California) even permit a division of spoils for living together.

Fourth, most states still have on the books century-old adultery laws, which proscribe that activity as a criminal offense.

The "complex" fact pattern that might otherwise serve as a maturation process therefore becomes a wonderful means for discussing how to screw one's lovers in the fashion of a law firm. The period of time together is assessed, along with any property brought into the "estate" during that period; the possibility of having received a sexual disease without yet having signs of it leads to another claim for damages; the appropriate share in the other's law license is subject to debate; and, if the other lover was married at the time, the threat of reporting the adultery to the D.A. can be used to ensure settlement and payment.

Perspiration

Perspiration is another important facet of the first year which separates the real lawyer from the imitator. Imitators are born with sweat glands under their arms, between their legs, and on their foreheads. When they are being grilled by a professor or an in-bred, or when the weather is hot (such as in late spring or early fall, for those who have forgotten about seasons), their sweat glands presage their eventual lack of success in the law.

Genetic lawyers are born without sweat glands. In their place, they have glands that secrete a mixture of powder and an odor that makes other people need to hand over money.

Study Groups

Law students also learn to work together as true lawyers. This process occurs in the study group. The study group is composed of one genius non-lawyer-to-be, three idiots, one nerd, and one lawyer-to-be. The genius answers all the questions. The idiots provide the food and entertainment. The nerd yells at the genius and the idiot. And they all ensure that the lawyer-to-be will be capable of bluffing himself into an A (the genius will get a B+, because he doesn't know how to bluff, and the rest will receive B's).

If the genius is stumped on a question and the lawyer-to-be either knows the correct answer or how to bluff a correct answer, the lawyer-to-be will give everyone else the wrong answer. This activity

43

is known as learning how to stab people who help you in the back. It is important in later life for surviving the process known as becoming a partner.

.Otherwise, study groups serve as cliques, just like cliques in junior high and high schools. "I belong to this study group" or "I'm off to my study group" are the intellectual mating calls heard echoing throughout hallways. Members of study groups cling together during coffee breaks in the lounge, research in the library, visits by or to

---

A LAW SCHOOL CHRONOLOGY -- MALE
Lawyer-Not-to-Be

First year, first semester
Extreme fear lightened with strong doses of nausea.
Inability to answer any questions.
Wild crushes on female students.
Study hours on end using assigned course books written by the professors.

First year, second semester
Extreme nausea lightened with strong doses of fear.
Inability to say anything other than a case name and date.
Begging women to marry.
Study hours on end using horn books.

First year, summer
Work as an auto mechanic.

Second year, first semester
Discover law ponies that synopsize an entire course in fifty pages, including exam questions and answers.
Discover that female students have been dating professors.
Discover the neighborhood bar.

Second year, second semester
Stop studying and worrying about women.
Go to summer job interviews around the clock.

---

parents, and sexual escapades. Study group members take notes for each other, prepare charts on possible test questions, and always sit in a circle so that their feet can touch.

First Summer

The summer at the end of the first year can be skipped by most students since most will not have law-related jobs. Those who do get law-related jobs receive them because: they are working in their fathers' law firms; they are working for a dollar fifty in a two man firm

---

Second year, summer
Work as a senior auto mechanic.

Third year, first semester
Worry about getting a law job paying more than interest due on student loan.
Marry a fellow student who remains friendly with a professor.
Stop going to classes.
Engrave name on stool at the bar.

Third year, second semester
Divorce, file counterclaims against ex-wife.

Interview around the clock.
Don't remember where the law school is.
Accept first offer.

Graduation, summer
Study for bar exam using a booklet synopsizing the law in ten pages.
Take bar exam in terrible neighborhood.
Get mugged.
Discover that he is still a child and that his mother drags him around the neighborhood upon his return home to tell everyone that he is a lawyer.
Reconcile with ex-wife since will be working eighty hour weeks anyway.

---

and have good measurements; they are genetic lawyers-to-be. Only the latter will net more than fifteen thousand dollars and will claim to have written a dozen memos which proved arcane points of law and won the cases. Their demeanor will have changed, too. They will attend second year classes wearing three-piece suits and will no longer raise their hands to answer questions; they will, instead, briefly wriggle their right wrists so that the light can reflect from their massive school rings. Sometimes, they will merely *harumph,* a sign that they had too many lunches with senior partners.

Second Year

The second year is a time for reassessing life. Which scotch is really the best? Which professor really has the most power and influence? Should I take Criminal Procedure II or Secured Transactions? Toward the end of the first semester, second year, it becomes apparent that law school should only be a year long, if that.

The real task during second year is to get a summer law job. As the genetic lawyer-to-be knows, interviewing for a law job means research. What he will do is find out the name of the interviewer, look him up in Martindale Hubbell (one of the Bibles of the industry, although not as good as hiring a detective; besides, lawyers pay to have full listings), various *Who's Who*'s (where one doesn't pay to be listed, although it is recommended that the volumes be purchased), and school directories. He will then phone home to find out if any of the lawyer's clients happen to be family members or friends.

He will discover as much as he can about the firm in a similar manner. He will not waste his time with firms that he knows will never hire him, or with firms that he wouldn't want to be caught dead in as a client. His final bit of research will entail memorizing a string of dirty jokes.

Everyone else, being nervous wrecks, will interview anywhere, anytime, from the small firms using telephone booths as offices to the large firms which might ask whether they would consider spending the summer as a paralegal's assistant. They will even look outside of firms, at government agencies, stuttering out that they want to consider "public interest" work.

This willy-nilly approach may result in call-backs to prestige firms where the truth of the matter is often presented. Blacks at all firms and Jews at old guard firms find themselves being stared at by everyone, from secretaries to bald partners, and the smiles and glints in the eyes are hardly ingratiating. Women, on the other hand, find that all eyes are at chest level when they are walking, and at knee level when they are sitting.

The lawyer-to-be will control the interview process. He will enter the room, shake hands firmly while staring down the partner, promptly select a seat, and then rearrange it. Interviewers have a number of tricks, such as putting the interviewee's chair at an angle away from the desk chair, or at an angle and twenty feet from the desk, or in direct sunlight. The true lawyer-to-be will immediately move the chair so that it faces where the interviewer will be sitting, is four feet away, and is out of any direct lighting or heat.

The interviewee will politely answer a few initial questions and then launch into a two minute discourse about the interviewer's distinguished background and the distinguished background of the law firm. He will note that Mr. Glundorff, the president of Duck Soup Industries and a major client of the firm, has sent his greetings, as he happens to be a family friend. He will mention that his cousin attended the same private school as the interviewer's daughter. After a solid but sibilant sigh, he will repeat how distinguished it all is. The interviewer will then lean back in his chair and hold forth for the remainder of the interview on how wonderful he and his firm are, while feeling out the student with regard to whether his family business might not consider a change in legal representation.

The student who will not succeed as a lawyer will be down the hall sweating furiously since his chair is in direct sunlight and next to the heating vent. His fingers will be shredding each other and it will seem as if everything he says is punctuated with loud burps. He will hear himself stumbling into an idiotic, heart felt discussion, as

What You Aren't Supposed To Know ...

follows:

PARTNER: Why did you select this firm?

MARVIN: I haven't selected it yet. I would like to keep all my options open.

PARTNER [*in disbelief*]: Then why are you here?

MARVIN: Oh, it's not that I don't want to work at your firm. It's that I want to feel out different firms. I'm looking for a certain type of milieu.

PARTNER: A milieu?

MARVIN: I would like to work with people who are open and intelligent and who look forward to a good legal challenge.

PARTNER: You know we do pro bono work.

MARVIN: That's not quite what I mean. I would like my work to count and not just be there for the billable hours. I would like to have an impact on society. I don't want to be just another body.

PARTNER: Well. I see from your resume that you are not on law review. Why is that?

MARVIN: You see, I'm a professional writer and I've already won the Pulitzer prize in non-fiction. I didn't want to waste my time doing cite checking.

PARTNER: That's your opinion of law review?

MARVIN: Yes.

PARTNER: You still haven't answered the question, though.

MARVIN: Which one?

PARTNER: I take it your grades weren't good enough to get on law review.

MARVIN: No. They were. As a matter of fact, I was asked. I turned them down because I've already won the ...

PARTNER: So you aren't on law review and you're entirely unsure as to why you would want to work at my firm?

MARVIN: I didn't say that. I said ...

The partner above, it must be pointed out, has an obligation to his firm to be very selective. Second year internships are used to assess associate potential, discussed below. He will harumph and form a church steeple with his fingers; he will swivel abruptly on his chair; he will stick a finger into an ear and rotate it with savage thought. With a lawyer not-to-be, he will either evince an immediate decision (as by closing his eyes), or will make it clear that the fact that he is going to take the matter into consideration is a tremendous favor on his part.

Classes

Second year classes are for the most part elective. For anyone with some legal experience by then, the absurdity of having professors who have never practiced law becomes even more pressing, since the tendency is to answer questions based upon actual experience instead of the theoretical qualities that teachers prefer. The teachers never see it that way; they see themselves as those who have written law review articles or treatises that have been cited by the United States Supreme Court in footnotes; as members of committees which have drafted laws that were later adopted; as practitioners who have, from time to time, offered their services (for a fee) as consultants on cases on appeal, or who have submitted friend-of-the-court briefs arguing their personal beliefs.

The genetic lawyer-to-be will ignore both reality and theory, since he is intent only on success. But the lawyer-not-to-be, who might have a part-time job as a law clerk for a judge or at a firm, will inevitably respond with his more realistic approach and be promptly shot down.

A LAW SCHOOL CHRONOLOGY -- FEMALE
Genetic Lawyer-to-Be

First year, first semester
Always raise hand in class.
Carry fifty pounds of books with ease.
Purchase blond wig.
Pursue professors.
Begin drafting a law review article.

First year, second semester
Always raise hand in class while shouting out answer.
Carry seventy-five pounds of books with ease.
Become assistant to tenured professor.
Hand in law review article
Accept job at father's law firm.

First year, summer
Work as law intern at father's law firm.

Second year, first semester
Organize study groups.
Have friends from study groups shepardize and re-write rejected law review article.
Sit primly in class since no longer need to answer questions.
Work part-time at a nearby law firm for a partner friendly with father.

Clinics

If "reality" is desired by a law student, he is supposed to participate in a clinic. Clinics are inevitably run by professors who recall their youths as hippies and insist that students watch *The Big Chill* before the first class. Clinics concentrate on two areas: class action suits, and representing the poor.

Class action suits are nice because the professor gathers together a group of people who claim to have been hurt by the same civil wrong. Since a group of people is involved, the suit can often gain media attention. Besides, a group increases the chances of

---

Second year, second semester
Reject numerous marriage proposals.
Date law review editor-in-chief.
Be accepted to law review.
Accept summer position at major firm where father used to work.

Second year, summer
Internship at one thousand dollars a week.
Attend numerous parties.
Have a fling with married partner on hiring committee.

Third year, first semester
Accept offer to return to large firm as associate.
Strike up strong friendships with professors since only student still attending class.
Publish law review article on the impact of sexual discrimination on socio-economic realities.

Third year, second semester
Take time off for a trip to Europe.

Graduation, summer
Arrange to take bar exam in Florence, Italy.

51

meeting available women. And there are lots of important issues amenable to class action status: access to cable television; getting a wider selection of pay cable stations; maintaining the fees for cable television.

Representing the poor can also have its media value. These cases usually entail joining forces with major law firms which are contributing efforts on a *pro bono* basis. Pro bono is said to mean "for [the] good," but notice it is not pro publico bono (for the public good). A more accurate translation of pro bono is "for profit or advantage," not only because that is its primary meaning in Latin, but also because that's exactly what it entails for clinic professors and the law firms. The media declares how wonderful it is that these poor people are finally receiving decent representation; in reality, the poor people are getting horrendously misplaced representation by people with no understanding of their needs or the legal procedures involved in pursuing their suits, while the law firms are receiving great, free advertising and the clinic professor is making contacts at the firms which might be economically fruitful at a later date.

The genetic lawyer-to-be will grasp these fundamentals immediately, and will ensure that his face turns up in every newspaper photograph. The other students will be given the library detail.

Planning For Honors

From second year on, the genetic lawyer-to-be will be conscientiously planning his route to receiving academic honors. Since those honors are based on grades, the genetic law student will select only those courses where the professors are known to grade easily, base grades upon a student's previous grades, or to give the same test each year (while keeping copies of previous tests on file in the library). Everyone else will be selecting courses based upon their interests or, at most, upon what they think a law firm would like to see on a resume.

Second Summer

Second year summer associates are tested in the following: drinking ability; eating and talking at the same time ability; country club ability; and bladder control.

Female associates are given further tests: breast size ability (through the use of wet T-shirt contests or pencils); ease of sex ability; and manner of dress ability.

Attractive female associates have the same summer story: "Partner X, who is married with three children he's never seen, asked me to have an affair with him during the summer. Partner X is on the hiring committee. What was I supposed to do? If I didn't fuck him, I knew he'd give me a bad review. If I did, it would set a pattern and, besides, he's short, ugly, and picks his nose."

The female associate who has to ponder the dilemma will not succeed as a lawyer, if only because she believes it's a dilemma.

The black summer intern is made to feel at home by being invited to parties held at discotheques where the four hundred white associates form a circle around him to see if he can really dance.

The genetic lawyer-to-be, however, has loads of fun. He is given theater tickets. Sometimes, he is given a business credit card and telephone service card. In major cities, he is often given a housing allowance, bringing his summer income of six to ten thousand up another four digits. He hobnobs with partners and senior associates, sitting in their offices drinking vodka and pineapple juice, sucking in the gossip and jokes and adding his own. Unlike the female associate fighting off the hiring partner's advances, or the lawyer-not-to-be stuck every night in the library, the genetic lawyer learns how to elevate his ability to bluff into a breezy attitude. He whisks about, his back straight, his head up, his hands ready to give a slap to an important shoulder, his lips prepared to smile prior to mentioning that the other summer associates just don't seem to be holding their own. Three weeks into the summer, he is offered a position at the firm for after graduation.

What is wonderfully pertinent about these summers of fun and innuendo is that the costs are passed through to clients.

What You Aren't Supposed To Know ...

Third Year

The third year of law school is a financial boon to law schools since no one attends classes by then. Its purpose is to test the student's ability to cope with boredom. This is more important than most students realize at the time because boredom is a large part of the practice of law.

The last semester of law school provides some entertainment in that it is a time for accepting positions offered from the summer internship or of desperately seeking a fulltime position. General interviewing techniques have already been discussed.

If you attend a ranked law school, you will be invited to parties given by the big law firms. These parties are held in moderately expensive restaurants and in a buffet style: open bar, open bar, and mounds of plump shrimp.

One story has it that a student and his wife attended a party held by one of the top firms in the country. The pair, being conventional, wore their wedding bands. By the time they arrived at the party, the genetic students had clamped onto the attending partners, the idiots were gobbling the shrimp, and the nerds were proving their alcoholic mettle. The duo meandered to the large table and began eating. A name partner from the firm wandered over and spent the ensuing fifteen minutes making passes at the wife amidst loud protestations from the student. The partner dragged her to a table to sit on his lap and tried fondling her. The student yelled at the partner and pulled her away. Two days after the incident, the student received a letter of rejection from the firm even though he had not yet had his first interview.

The third year of law school has two other events of note that are inevitable. A great many people marry, primarily from the fear that when they begin work they will never have the opportunity to socialize and woo again. And a great many already married female students will become pregnant and give birth exactly three weeks before final exams, last semester.

Bar Review And Exam

But -- is law school over with the cap and gown and pellucid speeches? Not at all, and I'm not talking about student loans looming on the horizon. If any additional proof was needed that 1) law school can be taught in a month, and 2) law school is irrelevant to the real world, it is what happens when one graduates. One then enters the world of bar review courses. Are these courses free, painless, and bookless? No. They are expensive, as boring as law school (in an accelerated way), and entail reading a number of oversized books.

As every lawyer discovers later in practice, practicing law means attracting every salesman in the galaxy. Insurance salesmen will be knocking on your door; so will bar associations; rental car agencies; commodities' brokers; in-laws. You name it. But the first hustle is the law review course. A law review course insists that it does what law school did not do, i.e., prepare you to take the state bar exam.

A state bar exam consists of a multistate multiple answer section; a state essay and multiple answer section; and a professional ethics section, also multistate.

In many states, the state part of the exam is not even looked at if the graduate receives a certain grade on the multistate. After all, who has the time to read thousands of essays scribbled in a lawyer's illegible handwriting? Since the multistate is multiple answer, and since it is asking questions supposedly involving general legal principles, one can note right off the bat that the odds favor a majority of students passing the exam. And that would be true of the majority of any grouping of students, or even apes or mice.

But,[9] assume you don't get a high enough grade on the multistate to pass solely on that. If you are a genetic lawyer, you will be able to bluff your way through any essay on the state exam. I don't think anyone looks at the ethics part of the exam. Certainly, it will never come up again except as a party joke.

Bar review courses are really tailored to the lawyer who will not succeed. After all, if things are going to go wrong, they are going to start with the bar exam. Such as not passing by one point.

A bar review course is taught in the seediest hotel in town. The

55

ballroom has massive chandeliers that creak directly overhead and have one working bulb that flickers. There is no ventilation. Large pitchers of iced water are provided "free," but there are no working toilets. The folding, metal chairs have plastic seat pads that glue themselves to your skin if you are wearing shorts. The long metal tables have long white table cloths decorated with cigarette holes. Far in the front of the room, where they cannot be seen, are the lecturers who are "experts" in each area of the law and who all try a different act to keep you awake.

The first session, you may be given a sample exam which everyone will fail (otherwise, what incentive to continue the course and not get a pro rata refund?). At the end of the course, you will take another sample exam which you will also fail. But by then you can't get a refund.

What I liked about my bar review course was that lecturers would preface their sessions with one of two phrases, either "Listen carefully because this will definitely be on the exam," or "We'll go through this quickly because it definitely won't be on the exam." Wonder of wonders, my lecturers were dead wrong. For example, the lecturer on criminal law insisted that degrees of crimes would never be on the essay section or short answer part of the state exam. He was right about the latter and wrong about the former. The first essay question asked for an analysis of a situation involving a variety of degrees.

As far as his being right about the short answer part, that was because the lecturer on domestic relations had insisted that Dom. Rel. would never be on the exam and, of course, the short answer part was sixty percent Dom. Rel. questions. Thank God I had just been through a divorce.

By the way, the seedy setting for the bar review is the only aspect relevant to the exam itself. Bar exams are held in condemned warehouses, condemned buildings, on wharves, anywhere students will have to fear for their lives getting there and home.

You enter one of the caverns to the sounds of dripping water and the chirruping of large shadowy creatures in the corners, and sit down at a clot of fibreboard termed a desk beneath a ceiling with no lighting at all except the sunlight creeping like excited motes between the holes in the roof. And you do that for three days.

One would surmise that, in this age of computerization and No. 2 pencils, you would be promptly notified of your passage (or failure) on your way to not becoming a partner. But the bar exam is regulated by lawyers and it will always rain on your one day off every ten years.

You take the bar exam (the first time) in the middle of the summer and will not hear your results until Thanksgiving. Why? Remember what was said before about law school courses and how they are always centered around meal times so that no one enjoys a meal? What better meal to destroy than Thanksgiving dinner?

If you are, in the meantime, adjusting to life in a large firm, odds are that not passing the bar exam will mean a pat on the back and a shove to the door. Some firms do let you try again, just once. Some places let you try as often as you like, but you will never see a salary increase and you know, deep down inside, that you are a marked person. In one large firm, half the paralegals are law school graduates who have not passed the bar. Of course, the other paralegals have passed the bar exam and are from unranked law schools.

Reciprocity

As matters still stand, becoming a member of a state bar means that you can become a member of federal district courts in your area. Does that mean you can step across the border and toot your legal horn, especially since you passed a "multistate" bar exam? No. You can attempt to argue a motion by seeking a temporary admittance to the court known as "Pro haec vice" and pronounced by lawyers as "Pro hike vishy." But most states follow a standard known as "lack of reciprocity" and most courts provide in local rules that a local attorney must be the attorney of record.

Lack of reciprocity is an important legal concept in that it protects state bars that consider themselves so much more erudite and intelligent than their neighboring lawyers. It means you cannot practice here unless you cough up another couple of hundred bucks and take our bar exam. If you have received a certain grade on the multistate, some states require you to take only the state's essay portion of the exam. Since those are the same states that generally do not read the state essay portion if you receive that same grade on the multistate, you can sense the absurdity in this. So some bar regulations provide for the rational exception: if you have practiced for, say, five years in your state and have not been disbarred or discovered with your pants down in an awkward situation, you can be waived into the bar of another state.

And what does that mean? Not much, since the second important legal concept is that You shall not come in here and take work away from our people. Thus, the local rules provide that local counsel with a local address must have a piece of the action. Although it will be the lawyer from State X, where the client is, who prepares the papers and argues the case, it will be the lawyer from State Y, where the court is, who will file the papers. Filing out-of-state papers is a lucrative business and logically requires a law degree for its proper handling. The fact that the papers could be filed by mail, or that they will be lost by the court clerk or the judge anyway, is irrelevant.

Footnotes:

1. Digressions are a means for adding pages otherwise unnecessary to an argument, primarily because the argument, standing alone, sucks. "Digression" originates from digressio, meaning to deviate.

2. Early morning professorial drunkenness is detected not so much by slurred speech as from an inability to control the tongue, which will often slip out of the mouth at inappropriate moments and dangle in an embarrassing fashion. That movement is sometimes confused with a certain sexual proclivity, but the motions are distinguishable. Whereas in the former, a lack of control is apparent, in the latter, complete control is present and the professor will not bite his tongue.

3. In the law, examples and cases abound and are often too numerous to mention. The phrase means either that no examples or cases exist, in which event they won't be mentioned, or that examples and cases, too numerous to mention, do exist, and will be mentioned forthwith.

4. Dom. Rel. is the abbreviation for Domestic Relations, which is the euphemism for pre-nuptial agreements and post-nuptial divorces. This is not to be confused with hiring maids.

5. The female law student who takes the side of the admitted rapist is revealing herself to be genetically born to the law. In most instances in Criminal Law class, however, students will merely giggle hysterically as they discuss rape, mayhem, dismemberment, torture and mass murder.

6. An in-bred attorney is the son or daughter of two genetic lawyers who are themselves descended from genetic lawyers. In-bred attorneys may or may not make it as lawyers, but are known to occasionally bite clients on the hand.

7. Not to dwell on ethnic events while doing so anyway, one interesting phenomenon in certain law schools is the Orthodox female law student who always seems to wear a Frederick's of Hollywood blond wig, a blouse open to her belly button, and jeans that are actually painted onto her. Dating one is just as interesting, in that you will be interviewed over the telephone by her brothers and her mother. These women are often referred to as the Sabbath Night Fever or Davaning Disco crowd.

8. Contingency fee lawyers accept a case for "free," i.e., they only get paid if they win the case. But if they do win the case (or settle it), their fee is huge and they can make a bundle as compared to the work put in. Bankruptcy lawyers who represent debtors or Creditors' Committees also work for "free" in the sense that they are only paid on an interim basis after applying

59

to the bankruptcy court for payment of their fees. Most law firms shun both contingency fees or bankruptcy applications for fees because they prefer billing the client up front.

9. Lawyers insist on overusing commas and semicolons. Whenever an adverb or conjunction is used, it is likely to be followed by a comma, as in "But, ..."; "Or, ..."; "Thus, ..." Those examples also serve to illustrate the use of semicolons.

CHAPTER THREE

LAW FIRMS

Types Of Firms

There are many different types of law firms in the big cities: downtown law firms, midtown law firms, law firms of extreme sizes (anywhere from one attorney to six hundred), specialty firms, transactional law firms, boutiques, and franchises.

Downtown law firms tend to be stodgy, historical, and old. By old, I mean that the partners have an average age of sixty; the messengers have an average age of seventy; the buildings still have bullet holes from the Revolutionary War; and there is solid wood everywhere. But when you look carefully at the rugs or the radiators or walls, you can see signs of decrepitude.

By historical is meant that when you first interview there and/or when you first appear as an associate for indoctrination, you are promptly led to the framed parchment next to the grandfather clock that shows the genealogy of the firm. The genetic lawyer's eyes will promptly shine with tears and he will bow his head in respect.

Midtown firms are supposedly more upbeat. They have plush industrial carpeting, wood veneers, modernistic paintings and sculpture, rows and rows of plants, bright young secretaries, and an average partner age of fifty-two. But don't let the lower age fool you. It is due to partner turnover. Every year, a few partners from each midtown firm will split off and form their own firms. The genetic lawyer knows the importance of being what is known as a "name" partner (otherwise, lawyers are just lawyers without any names, just billing numbers).

Downtown firms are blond and blue eyed. Midtown firms are brown haired and brown eyed. You will find one or two blacks in each of the larger firms. It used to be that they were placed way in the back of the firm, where construction was always in progress, but lately I have noticed that black attorneys are permitted to use the front entrance.

Downtown firms used to be the largest firms. Many of them were dependent upon one or two institutional clients for their entire billings. During the recession and the big antitrust settlements with major corporations, many of those firms ended up in a bind that meant releasing flocks of associates to the streets. Some of the downtown firms are in a period of resurgence, bringing in entire departments, particularly in bankruptcy, real estate, and venture capital.

The same time period that wreaked financial ruin on many of the downtown firms permitted the midtown firms to expand rapidly, particularly in real estate, bankruptcy, and general litigation. One firm that grew to a particularly astronomical size during this period was Finley, Kumble, et al.[1] The firm then exploded, spewing forth the guts of hundreds of suddenly unemployed associates into the byways of the universe. The partners, of course, promptly set up independent firms or joined other firms, and everyone sued everyone else over lost pay, profits, and liability for the dead firm's debts. So it is with the ups and downs of firms.

The other types of firms first mentioned are usually small and partner heavy, meaning one will find ten to fifteen partners, most of whom have been brought in laterally from other small offices. There may be one to two associates per partner, but that number is illusory in that associate turnover will be extremely high.

A specialty firm, in this context, is one which advertises itself as practicing primarily one type of law. The firm might declare, for example, that it practices "computer law." In reality, the firm is hoping to build a practice in that area, but in the meantime it will be a small case general practice firm, taking on foreclosures, car thefts, and collection matters.

Boutiques are firms which have seen better days, perhaps even reaching the 100-lawyer mark before shrinking rapidly. Since their names might still have some luster left over from their heydays, these firms attempt to recoup clients by modeling themselves after the shopping mall concept. That is, no client is too small, no matter too simple, and all clients and matters can be handled in one sitting. Bring in the entire family and we will write out your wills, trusts, incorporation papers, and complaints.

Franchises use a similar concept except that on top of wills and divorces, the client can step next door to get eyeglasses and shoes. Franchises have started using so-called specialists to handle intricate matters, but in the main, these storefronts hire litigators at low salaries. These lawyers are given a carrot in that if they turn out enough cases for enough time, they will be granted increasing percentages of the take. The bulk of the work involves individual bankruptcies, uncontested divorces, filing incorporation papers, and suing individuals for small amounts of money.

Another type of firm calls itself transactional, which means that the client gets to meditate on his bill in a dark conference room.

Departments

Medium to large sized law firms are departmentalized. The core departments are litigation (sometimes including bankruptcy), corporations, and real estate. The fringe departments are tax, and trusts and estates (T&E). If there is a white collar crime department (currently the up-and-coming specialty in the position bankruptcy was a few years ago), it usually consists of one extremely odd partner who spends half his time staring at the wall muttering to himself and the other half listening to shadowy clients wearing sunglasses.

The genetic associate recognizes that different departments have different sources of political power. There are a number of rules of thumb involved here. T&E departments can be dispensed with right away. They are very small and are kept as a favor to elderly clients. T&E is sometimes jokingly referred to as tits and estrogen, since the department attracts women who rapidly age to look like their clients.

White collar crime departments, as departments of one partner, are actually very powerful nowadays because many white collar

LAW FIRM DEPARTMENTS

Litigation: Often one of the largest in numbers, but subject to tremendous fluctuation because dependent on referrals from other departments. Litigators are under the inventory classification FIFO: first in, first out. Litigators file tremendous quantities of papers to force the government to build new courthouses. Most litigators never go to court.

Corporate: Also one of the largest departments and usually the department of choice because it is like running a publishing house. A corporate lawyer files incorporation papers and has the corporate book printed up and bound. He files required papers, printed and bound, with the Securities and Exchange Commission. He drafts long memos with appropriate appendices, exhibits, and bibliographies, which are bound with a typeset cover. Unlike litigators, corporate lawyers are given their own business cards and attractive secretaries.

Bankruptcy: With the exception of a few specialized firms, usually one of the smaller departments. Often lumped in with the litigation department. Bankruptcy lawyers are considered a "club," which still has connotations of being the legal rat pack. The main purpose of bankruptcy lawyers is to become lead counsel to any one of the number of committees set up to ensure the gutting of the bankrupt entity. Other than that, bankruptcy lawyers spend their time petitioning the court for payment of fees from the estate.

Real Estate: Size follows real estate booms. Most of real estate practice involves attendance at closings. Since almost all of the closing papers will be from the bank that will carry the mortgage, and the bank will never renegotiate its clauses, a lawyer at a closing will try to look busy by xeroxing the checks handed over by the client to the bank.

Trust and Estates: Usually a small department of old attorneys who dress in black. Since drafting a will or a trust is no big deal, the primary purpose of T&E lawyers is to lobby state and federal legislatures so that laws affecting trusts and deaths are changed on an annual basis, requiring a redrafting of all those will and trusts.

Tax: Also a small department since no one in their right mind would try to advise anyone else on how to file a tax return.

Domestic Relations: A small department provided as a service to clients who need to be riled up every now and then into an intense hatred of their spouses.

Labor/ERISA: Primarily the latter, which involves the complexities of certain pension plans that no one comprehends.

Intellectual Property: One of the up-and-coming departments, but the name is a misnomer. It does not mean property that is intelligent, such as the pet cockatoo. Nor does it mean computers, which are too intelligent. It really means filing patents, trademark registrations, copyright registrations, and then threatening to sue anyone whose machine, trademark, or book seems to be infringing.

Computer Law: The technological bandwagon, in that all attorneys now say that they practice computer law. In other words, they will put the word "computer" or "CPU" into a standard lease, contract, or security agreement. Ask them about megahertz, cost per byte, RAM drives, syntactical differences in high level languages, or how to turn a machine on, and they will stutter that those are business decisions, having nothing to do with the law.

clients are very powerful and wealthy (and, if the partner wins the case, the clients will remain very powerful and wealthy). As a source of political power within the firm, however, the departments are weak because their partners are perceived as being mavericks. White collar partners tend to be the exception to genetic lawyers -- because of the nature of their practice, they can get away with a lot. A problem that has arisen, though, is that under some new laws, money paid to a lawyer which is traceable back to illicit activities can be retrieved by the federal government. For that reason, white collar crime attorneys now demand payment in advance -- and in unmarked bills.

Litigation departments have grown tremendously in recent years, but the departments are cyclical and can shrink just as rapidly. Litigators tend to have very little political power because litigators are referred clients, they do not have clients. Litigators are known as the "dime a dozen" crowd.[2]

One recent exception is the growth in bankruptcy filings, especially by huge corporations that are not bankrupt but wish to avoid threatened liability for their nefarious acts. Bankruptcy departments are generally listed as being part of the litigation department, although bankruptcy partners prefer to work "behind the scenes" and push litigation partners into the courtroom. In half the cases, bankruptcy partners have their own client base. In the other half, cases are "referred" from the corporate department (think about that one for a moment). Bankruptcy partners that have their own institutional clients tend to have power within a firm. The one caveat is that bankruptcy is still considered a rat's game that attracts sleazy attorneys. This perception is, in many instances, correct. At the least, bankruptcy lawyers tend to be clubbier than other groupings of attorneys and will think nothing of screwing a non-bankruptcy lawyer who invades their territory.

Corporate departments are the bread and butter departments for many firms. A firm's clients usually originate with corporate partners. Since corporate work involves millions of pages of forms, corporate partners are known to make mistakes at times, primarily from intense boredom. It is those mistakes that are termed "referrals" to the litigation department.

Tax departments are typically small and most associates have an L.L.M. in tax. An L.L.M is a graduate degree granted by most law schools; admissions to these programs is open door -- all one has to do is pay, and deduct.

Tax departments exist on referrals from the corporate departments. Tax departments do negative work. If the Tax Code says X, how can I work it so my client can do not-X and get away with it?

Real estate departments used to be minor departments until the real estate boom of the mid-1980's. Many real estate departments became as large as litigation departments. Real estate partners have their own clients and "refer" a number of matters to the litigation department. In contrast to bankruptcy, where the attorneys are considered the slime of the earth, real estate departments are stereotyped as having the slimiest clients, such as your neighborhood slumlord. Once the boom faded, real estate departments became dispensable and their members turned to what they really wanted to do -- form investment groups for the production of violent, sexy, low-budget motion pictures in Malaysia.

A domestic relations attorney probably has the hardest legal job in the sense of maintaining a semblance of rationality. Couples who are divorcing or battling for custody are not known for their equanimity. Nor are the judges assigned to family courts known for their graciousness or erudition. On the other hand, dom. rel. attorneys are themselves known to feed off the emotional blood of a divorce proceeding, knowing that they can inflate bills with meaningless work because the client will be exhausted from the proceedings.

Private union attorneys have it easier than anti-union attorneys in the sense that the latter often do not survive the picket line they must cross on their way to confer with their clients. But private union attorneys must suffer in American-made clothes and cars while their counterparts wear designer suits and drive Mercedes Benz's.

What You Aren't Supposed To Know ...

First Year Associates

The genetic associate is immediately attracted to corporate law. The power is there, the country club set is there, the work is relatively simple (although repetitive and boring), and the hours are short.

Litigation departments were established for the S&M crowd. The hours are extremely long (in fact, unending), the tension always growing, the loss of reality intense. Genetic associates who are stupid enough to go into litigation first -- mainly with dreams of oratory before a judge and jury who immediately recognize their brilliance -- usually try to switch into corporations.

Unless you are a genetic lawyer, however, it is extremely difficult to switch from a department after practicing for one year, with the exception that you can always switch to litigation. Lawyers get stamped early on both by department and by an area of specialization (which means you worked on one type of matter once and, therefore, will work on the same matters forever).

Offices

Most large firms and some small firms pride themselves on providing first year associates with their own office, although not necessarily close to a department the associate may have already selected. The office is usually six feet by six feet -- just large enough for a desk, lateral files, a desk chair, and a guest chair. Each office has one window. In a midtown firm, the windows cannot be opened, so that the associate is at the mercy of the partner down the hall who controls the temperature in his area.

The remaining firms stuff from two to six associates into offices measuring ten feet by ten. Nothing tests one's mettle more than being in an unventilated room during the peek of the summer heat wave with a group of associates who are: nervous; having digestive trouble after gulping down hot dogs and seltzer; pumping breast milk for their babies; menstruating; talking to themselves. Whoever emerges alive goes on to become a second year associate.

Secretaries

First year associates generally share a secretary with a partner. This means that a first year associate has no secretary. It is not that partners have a great deal of legal work, but that they have a great deal of personal work and, if the secretary is attractive, a great deal of dictation.

As a first year associate soon discovers, his memorandum due the next day will not be touched until the partner's bills have been paid, the partner's coffee cup cleaned, and the partner's weekend plans arranged. Since the memorandum inevitably ends up not being completed in time, the associate will find himself in hot water with the supervising partner.

The genetic lawyer will have thought of this problem beforehand and dated the office manager so that he can have her field out his work to other secretaries. The lawyer who will not succeed will type his own memoranda, thereby gaining the reputation of someone who types his own work (i.e., not partnership material), as opposed to someone who does what has to be done.

Party All The Time

Another perk provided by law firms is public (as opposed to private) drinking. This occurs weekly at cocktail parties, and semi-annually at the Christmas party and the firm outing.

A firm cocktail party is held in a conference room, typically beginning at five p.m. on a Friday afternoon. The party is catered in the sense that there will be bread, potato chips, dips, and perhaps sandwich squares with the crusts cut off. The genetic attorney will inevitably appear at six p.m., rushing in with his shirt sleeves rolled up and his tie partly undone as if he has just completed a mindboggling legal task. He will also make sure that he will be paged on the loudspeaker system or otherwise called to the telephones that are ubiquitous in every corner of a law firm. When he takes a phone call, he will hold the receiver to his face and utter astonishing sounds that imply

SALARIES AND BILLING

First year lawyers in many large firms take home about $70,000 in salary, bonuses, and incentives. Assuming that a lawyer bills 65 hours a week and takes only a one week vacation, then

3,315 hours into $70,000 equals $21.12 per hour,

which is not much more than what many union laborers, such as train conductors, make.

Assuming that the firm bills out the lawyer at $100 per hour and all of the billed hours are paid for, then the law firm grosses

3,315 times $100 equals $331,500,

which gives the law firm a net of

$331,500 minus $70,000 equals $261,500.

Since firms bill out most overhead to clients -- including secretarial time, and air conditioning or heating on weekends and after five on weekdays -- and disbursements such as meals, taxis, copying, and messengers, the only real overhead cost of an associate is office space and benefits. Since an associate pays a large percentage of benefits and pension plans never vest before an associate is dumped, and since the associate is clumped in with five other associates in a ten by ten office, then overhead for each associate can be estimated at

$1,000

leaving a net net profit to the law firm of

$260,500.

Under this scenario, a first year associate would have worked enough to pay back the firm's investment in him a bit after his first week on the job.

Obviously, the above is not what a law firm would want to admit. The primary objection is that a large percentage of a first year associate's billable hours will not be billed (uh huh). The reality is that not all associates will bill 65 or 70 hours a week, and that a majority of partners will not bring in the billable clients sufficient to cover their overall take (where take is not based on one's own clients). Moreover, senior associates and partners live in spacious rooms and partners are allocated annual furniture allowances.

To be on the safe side, then, I think one could accurately estimate that first year associates, on the average, have a pay-back period of two and a half months, with the remainder being net profit to the firm.

Taking into account salary increases over the years, with proportionate increases in the billed rate of the associate, one can estimate that a firm, over a seven year period, will net about one million dollars from an associate before he or she is let go.

THAT FIRST TOUR OF THE LAW FIRM

When a partner takes a potential associate on a tour, the inevitable stop at the bathroom always turns into an issue of aggrandizement.

"See here," he says proudly, "unlike those other large firms, we have individual glass stalls, fixtures imported from Italy, tiles imprinted with the names of partners, an electric shoe shiner for when it is too late to have the shoe shine boy come around, and a microwave. The towels are always lemony fresh."

At another firm, the topper will be the telephones in each stall, or the legal pads and pens over the toilet tissue, or the around-the-clock attendant (who still expects a tip).

And then there is the cafeteria. The cafeterias are like any other cafeterias. The trays are orange plastic. The tuna fish is watery and has celery in it. The difference is that you are handed a chit on the way in and if you write in the number for a client, you don't have to pay for it.

that he is handling a most delicate matter that will have tremendous financial benefits for the firm. When he hangs up the telephone, he will walk, still nodding his head, to the closest powerful attorney, grab his elbow, and whisper into his ear.

These calls are, of course, from the wife telling him to bring home a loaf of bread. Coming late to the party also means nothing more than that he fell asleep in his office from too much liquor during the day and forgot to set his alarm clock.

The lawyers who will not succeed will stand in corners sipping the wrong drink while no one pages or calls them.

At some firms, a game that is played weekly at cocktail parties is taking bets on how long it will take Partner X to drink enough to fall off his chair. This will always occur when Partner X is in the middle of a gloriously obscene story that, unfortunately, he never finishes.

Firm Outings

The firm outing occurs in the spring and involves going to a country club. The outing is only for the attorneys. Again, the genetic lawyer will appear late, out of breath, with pleadings, documents, 10-Ks, and paralegals falling from his pockets as he huffs to where the partners are congregated, sipping drinks and eating shrimp. Again, he will be paged, telephoned, called, sought after, and generally brought to the attention of the partners. He will be the one who tries for the impossible volleyball shot; plays doubles with the most powerful partner who has the worst tennis game; and who writes the skit and plays the lead role which sets all the partners laughing uncontrollably. After his shower and change, he will appear impeccably dressed in a tuxedo and polished shoes. During the course of the evening, he will be seated at the table with the name partners and will dance with their wives. He will tell wonderful jokes and then, his voice lower, discuss how terrible other associates are and what great work he has been doing.

The non-genetic attorney will sit in a corner sipping the wrong drink, unnoticed by the partners until one, mistaking him for a

WHAT AN HONESTLY ITEMIZED BILL WOULD LOOK LIKE

For professional services rendered:

Partner X, Sr. Associate Y initial conference with client, including telling jokes, asking about families, and then mentioning the matter, which is worth about $50,000 in lost revenue to the client   2 hours

Partner X, Sr. Associate Y conference about the matter, including jokes, discussions of family members, discussions as to who has the best looking secretary, decision as to how many junior associates and paralegals to put on the matter 4 hours

Partner X, Sr. Associate Y, Associates A, B, C: conference wherein matter was described once again, work fielded out, and lunch plans made to further discuss the matter 4 hours

Partner X describing matter with Partner E, who has no suggestions as to how to handle the case but points out that Partner G has just had his office refurnished and is spending a lot of time with female Associate R   1 hour

Luncheon with Partner X, Sr. Associate Y, Associates A, B, C to discuss matter briefly prior to ordering first round of drinks to be followed by wine, nouvelle cuisine and brandy 3 hours

Associates A, B, C do research and initial drafting, reporting in to Sr. Associate Y   12 hours

Supper with Partner X, Sr. Associate Y, Associates A, B, C and by special invitation Associate R wherein research and drafting are discussed during first round of drinks and then forgotten during fourth round of drinks   4 hours

Associates A, B, and C stay at firm all night waiting for word processors to print out a readable draft; Sr. Associate Y and

Associate R discuss matter at discotheque; Partner X meets with
secretary to discuss drafting of letter to client   24 hours

Client calls Partner X to say that matter has been settled
                                                    15 minutes

Time breakdown	Billed/hr.	Sub-Totals
Partner X -- 42 1/4 hrs.	$300	$12,675
Partner E -- 1 hr.	300	300
Sr. Ass. Y -- 53 hrs.	190	10,070
Ass. A -- 47 hrs.	150	7,050
Ass. B -- 47 hrs.	130	6,110
Ass. C -- 47 hrs.	110	5,170
Ass. R -- 28 hrs.	100	2,800
Secretary -- 53 hrs.	35	1,855

Disbursements:

Meals	$950
Taxis	120
Xeroxes	223
Messengers	85
Long distance telephone calls	45

Total Due:	$57,453

*Your patronage and prompt payments
are always appreciated!!!*

waiter, asks him to shine his shoes.

There are three main events at these gatherings. The first is ogling the female associates in their bikinis as they lounge around the pool.

The second are the speeches by the partners as to how great the firm is doing.

The third is the dancing where bets are taken as to whether the breasts of the female associates will bounce out of their low cut gowns.

Sometimes, the firm outing is broken up so that the country club is one aspect, a dinner/dance at an expensive hotel another, and dinner on a partner's terrace or in his backyard a third. What occurs is the same, however.

Christmas Party

The firm Christmas party is typically a time when both support staff and attorneys hobnob together. The food and liquor are not the best and the place where it is held is not the most exquisite. In any event, fun and games abound in that certain attorneys are bound to get drunk enough to make passes at certain secretaries.

Billing

Now that we have the departments and some accoutrements of the law straight, let's take a look at the most important aspect of first year training: Billing. Partners have code numbers and when they bring a matter in, the client is given a number, the matter is given a number, and the partner's code is listed beneath. You thought you had trouble enough learning your social security and phone numbers; look forward to memorizing client numbers.

An associate working on a case has three pieces of paper he can fill out with regard to billing: the diary (a sheet of paper with lines across it); the Lawyer's Diary (a bound book where each page

TYPICAL LAW FIRM PRO BONO CASES

Defending the senior or managing partner in a dog bite case.

Drafting wills for other lawyers in the firm.

Attending closings for other lawyers in the firm.

Prosecuting cases on behalf of one's own church, temple, or anti-discrimination association.

Joining one's coop or condo board.

Contesting anything frivolous on constitutional grounds.

Working for a political candidate who is in a position to appoint judges.

Doing tax returns for partners and their mistresses.

Arranging art exhibits for mistresses of partners.

Playing tennis or racquet ball with sons and daughters of important clients.

Contesting the parking tickets of partners on constitutional grounds.

represents one day; in the back is important information, such as attorneys in the area, judges, courts, a map of the world, and average rainfalls); and time sheets, which are three or four different colored sheets of paper that make carbon impressions (one sheet goes to accounting, one is kept for the associate's records, and the rest probably go to a paper shredder).

The genetic lawyer, like a fish taking to water, already knows that overbilling is the way of life. A mistake is underbilling. Underbilling means that you work on a matter for ten hours and you take off two hours that you feel were unproductive. Partners like to say to associates: "You bill. I'll decide whether to shave the time." Time, in the law, has whiskers.

Overbilling means including the two hours plus time spent in the bathroom, on the phone getting the correct time, gazing out the window, or scratching your crotch. All time is valuable and has to be paid for by someone. The client is that someone.

Overbilling is also fomented by the structure of law firms. Most law firms count the hours billed by associates and desire a set minimum such as two thousand hours a year. If your law firm has cots in the back, the minimum is probably twenty-seven hundred hours a year. If you have cots, shower stalls, and an in-house cafeteria, forget it; just multiply 365 by 24 and then add 1,000.

An associate who stars is usually a top biller. Top billers are also lucrative to the firm, assuming the client pays, since after the first quarter of the fiscal year (if that), all billings are pure profit to the firm.

Padding the bill is different from overbilling. Padding is where the client is in the Fortune 500, or is a client who was a referral who will never be seen again, or is a client suffering from Altzheimer's Disease. What it means is that when the time sheets are totaled, the partner adds on a number of hours.

Billing also serves the purpose of creating a record in the event of a malpractice suit. For that reason, time records themselves are typically exaggerated in terms of what was really done. For example, instead of jotting down, "Spoke to C.R. and he refused to give extension, thereby putting us in hot water. 2 hours," one jots down,

"Spoke to C.R. and took hard stand that will give us strategic advantage. 4 hours."

Genetic lawyers have a separate diary in which they jot down notes useful later on, when they are up for partnership. Such as, "Spoke to Partner X who mentioned he liked chocolate ice cream and that he had porked Secretary Y two years ago and had an illegitimate child by her. Pays support in cash on Wednesdays at 10."

Clients, of course, see none of these notes. Back in the good old days, bills were often brief: "For services rendered $25,000.00." Nowadays, clients have begun demanding itemized bills. An itemized bill reads as follows:

> For legal services rendered:
> Drafting of memoranda, correspondence, confer-
> ences, meetings $25,000.00
>
> Messengers   50.00
> Supplies   250.00
> Disbursements   500.00
> Other   1,000.00
>
> **TOTAL DUE** $47,235.34

If the client is institutional, such as a bank, odds are it won't question the bill and will promptly pay it. In one instance, a partner sent out two copies of the same bill and the client paid each. After the double payment had been discovered by the firm, an entire day was spent in conference trying to decide what to do -- and who, other than the partner, should take the blame.

What happens if a client does not pay a bill? The attorney gets an automatic lien on the client's papers. If a client is stupid enough to give an attorney original documents instead of xeroxes, and to not ask for copies of every memorandum and filing the lawyer makes during the course of a case, not having access to papers can be deadly.

Nonbill Time -- The Pro Bono Dog Case

Lawyers also get to record "nonbill" time. That means time spent where the "client" either does not exist, as in bar association work, or where the client exists but won't be paying, as in litigating a dog bite case for a partner. Partners love to sue their neighbors up in Westchester and places like that.

Every now and then an associate might be asked to take on a pro bono case. The question is typically phrased as follows: "Look, the Bar has been on our back because the firm hasn't handled a pro bono for the last ten years and it seems it's our turn. I want you to handle this one but remember it can't cut into your regular work load." (The true meaning of pro bono was discussed in the previous chapter, for those who missed that part.)

Pro bono cases can be a great deal of fun. One that I had involved a prisoner who had brought a certain type of federal action permitted against state prison officials. This prisoner, who had plea bargained to aggravated assault (probably of his former attorney), had been tested for drugs and tossed into the hole without the proper hearing required pursuant to prison regulations. It was not a bad case. I had to track down the prisoner through the prison system, since he was being moved from place to place with unusual rapidity. Finally, I spoke to the prisoner a few times on the telephone (the prison was in one of those places that is inaccessible except by helicopter and canoe and the firm was not about to spend money on those), did a great deal of research, and drafted the appropriate papers. At which time I was called by the head of the prison who asked me whether I had bumped into my Mr. X. I said no, why? He said because Mr. X had escaped and his last words had been that he was going to "check in" with his lawyer.

But for the most part, pro bono cases are ranked as follow: cases which will yield free advertising for the firm; cases on behalf of partners and their families; cases on behalf of one's own family; cases on behalf of religious or ethnic organizations; cases involving sexy women; cases involving animals; cases for people actually in need.

Associates And Illusory Client Cuts

An extremely interesting event occurs when an associate brings in a client. Law firms have an unwritten code (law firms will never put anything in writing involving their internal promises) that an associate who brings in a client will receive a percentage of the overall fees. This percentage is usually based on a sliding scale. But it can amount to a great deal of money. Partners will pull out every trick in the book to prevent an associate from getting his split.

For example, one associate who was a lateral transfer spent a year and a half socializing with a client of his former firm and finally reached the point where the potential client wanted to meet with a partner of his new firm. The meeting took place, the partner was given some piece work to do as a trial run, and the associate went out and bought a car based on his expected cut. Of course, no cut was allocated. As the partner put it, "What do you mean you brought in the client? I had the meeting, didn't I? I was given the work, wasn't I? You weren't offered any of those during the year you claim you proselytized them, were you?"

In another case, an associate built up his own reputation as an expert in a particularly arcane area. A genetic lawyer knows that an associate never reveals an expertise in any area a partner does not understand, which means most areas of the law. In this instance, the associate slid into his expertise perhaps without realizing it. The result, however, was that one of the partner's clients, having worked successfully with the associate, had another corporation's in-house counsel call the associate (and not the partner -- another affront) to work on a case requiring that expertise. The associate approached the partner with the new matter.

The partner's initial reaction was that the new matter could not be taken on. The partner detailed a number of reasons: a conflict of interest because of his client; the associate was overworked; the firm was overbooked. None of those excuses was true, so the partner then relied on his ultimate weapon. He told the associate he could not have the case.

The associate, who will not succeed as a lawyer, went above the partner's head to other partners in the firm who, smelling money, agreed to bring in the new matter. The associate, for his part, smelled money in his up-coming percentage.

Once the matter was finished to the entire satisfaction of the new client, the associate approached the partner with regard to his expected cut. The partner put him off a few times with a wave of the hand. Finally, the partner stated that the associate was not going to get a cut because the new client had come in through the recommendation of the partner's client. Therefore, the partner deserved the credit. Since most new clients come into a firm through recommendations from firm clients, the translation is that an associate who does an excellent job that attracts the attention of clients and induces them to suggest the associate to other potential clients will not only not get a pat on the back, he will receive a negative mark from the threatened partner. The moral: do bad work and stay in the background.

The Free Ride

After all, an associate should be satisfied with the fact that he will never have to buy breakfast, lunch or dinner again and that he will have transportation by cab to his doorstep every evening. The unwritten code in firms is this: if you have to be at work during a meal, charge a client for the meal; if you go out for a meal and discuss a matter, charge the client, even if the discussion takes only two seconds; if you "work" past eight p.m., take a cab home and charge the client (the only record will be that you were in a cab at eight fifteen). As one partner put it: "What we used to do was go out for a nice meal at six thirty, then drift back to the office at eight and call up the cab company."

Similarly, if you work on a matter that calls for you to travel to another city, you may not be able to fly first class, but you can drink a hundred tiny bottles of vodka and charge that to the client. And you can charge X-rated films shown in your plush hotel to the client, too, since that will only show up as a disbursement. A number of attorneys even get away with charging prostitutes visited in various cities to the client.

About the only thing an attorney cannot charge to a client outright or deduct from his own taxes are the dozens of gray and blue pinstriped suits, black socks, and black shoes that are the uniform of a high-powered lawyer. But that expense is made up for by raiding the firm's stock of supplies for stationery, folders, papers, and pens.

But a fledgling associate soon wakes up to the fact that he is in a class of twenty or thirty attorneys, and only one has a secure future.

What You Aren't Supposed To Know ...

Footnotes:

1. Et al. stands for et alia or alii, depending upon which crossword puzzle you do. It means "and others." Its primary purpose is to permit the addressing of an envelope to a law firm, since listing a firm's entire series of names typically requires seven envelopes.

2. Since the vast majority of lawyers will never spend a day in a courtroom (even assuming they could find a court), litigators are frowned upon as odd balls. This is a mistaken perception, since the vast majority of litigators don't want to spend a day in a courtroom either. Most cases are paper cases, i.e., a round of papers is followed by some discovery, a deposition or two, and perhaps a motion involving a three minute oral argument. If a case is actually put down for trial and the date cannot be adjourned, it will be settled. Some small firms specializing in actual trial practice achieve extremely favorable settlements because their attorneys know that most major firm litigation partners have never gone to trial and will do literally anything to avoid their first, even sell out their client's claim. When a law school professor settled his cable TV antitrust suit with Cravath, Swaine & Moore (297 lawyers), the professor and others termed it a major victory since the settlement gave them what they wanted. Cravath, meanwhile, claimed that the settlement was its victory. The Cravath partner on the case declared, "We didn't give up anything we weren't prepared to do anyway." Reported in Manhattan Lawyer, vol. 1, no. 15, Jan. 5 - Jan. 11, 1988, p. 4. Of course, one year of billable paper pushing, discovery, and depositions had transpired prior to settlement.

CHAPTER FOUR

DRAFTING AT FIRMS

Legal Research

An associate at a large firm will spend his first year sitting in the library. This is known as the "research" period. It is also a time for discovering the wonders of hemorrhoids.

Firms devote funds to libraries depending upon the senior partner's literacy and his niece's sense of interior design and decor. Some older firms have libraries that are in two tiers, which not only provide associates with exercise but also vantage points from which to leap. Newer firms seem to prefer the glass-enclosed library, which permits attorneys to see who is leaning over a book and who is resting his head on the book. But most libraries are like this: too small for shelving all the books, too few work tables, and chairs that would be rejected by the Salvation Army.

Firms differ in their research approaches. Some partners insist that all research begin with the King's Bench and English common law, thereby making law school relevant for a brief moment.

Other partners are aware of things called Records on Appeal, which makes research fun because you learn firsthand how the law is really practiced. A Record on Appeal is a bound book containing most of the papers and pleadings involved in a court appeal. You get a chance to read the memoranda from below and above, along with the lower court decision (often unpublished).

This shows you a number of things: 1) many memoranda are copied verbatim (except for a change in facts and caption) from memoranda previously filed by other firms in cases involving the same legal issue; 2) unpublished lower court opinions are either a handwritten paragraph or a long, rambling discourse saying nothing;

and 3) most appellate level opinions have nothing to do with the lower court decision or what is being briefed.

The majority of partners will remember nothing about research and will view it merely as a means for bloating the billable hours attributable to their cases. One way of doing this is by having an associate use computerized legal research. Computerized research is a failsafe method for increasing billed time in that: 1) the attorney selects the key words to be researched in the database; 2) no attorney knows anything about computer programs and their optimal use; 3) the attorney will inevitably select those key words that are common to all cases; and 4) the cost of a computer search is based upon time plus the frequency in which a key word appears in each case. On top of that, the associate, having pulled up two thousand cases containing his key words will then scan them on the terminal, or have them xeroxed by a paralegal, or look at each of them himself in the various reporters.

Regardless of the method of research selected, billable time and disbursements will be exponentially increased because the partner will insist that every single case be xeroxed at least in duplicate. An associate will learn later in life that everything under the sun has already been researched in every firm and all cases have been xeroxed at least a trillion times.

Memoranda

The approach to research fits right in with the concept of "bluffing." The genetic associate will draft a forty page memorandum containing one cite and two hundred footnotes and a genetic partner will be extremely content. The non-genetic law review associate will draft a forty page memorandum containing two thousand impeccable cites and two hundred footnotes and the genetic partner will be displeased. The associate who will never succeed will draft a ten page memorandum with one footnote and containing only the most recent and highest court opinions, but will also make the mistake of pointing out that the problem at hand touches on issues

THE ART OF NARROW RESEARCH

What Lawyers are:

Supposed to do	Actually do
Research completely and accurately.	If at Legal Aid or the D.A.'s office, rely on canned briefs; if at a major firm, rely on treatises.
Quote cases in context.	Quote out of context.
Cite adverse cases.	Ignore adverse cases.
Prepare questions in advance for computerized, billed searches.	Just fiddle around.
Not confuse the issue by citing cases from other states, worlds or universes.	Cite anything favorable, regardless of source.
Not declare a case what it is not.	Declare the only favorable case from the lowest court of a foreign state as the leading case, setting precedents.
Not declare the most recent U.S. Supreme Court decision on the issue a piece of malarky that need not be followed.	Cite Robert Bork.

such as the rule against perpetuities. The genetic partner will go through the roof.

All partners will at some point during a research project say one of the following:

1) Find a quote in a case that says "............." [giving a quote that is directly on point and favorable and which, of course, does not exist because no judge ever wrote it.]

2) I believe that Cardozo once said "............." Go lexis all Cardozo cases. [Mead Data should give a discount on that one since it's been run so many times. But, then again, it's the client who pays for it, so who cares?]

3) I don't like this decision [from the highest court in the relevant jurisdiction]. I know it clearly says that we have no case, but I think you can distinguish it if you give it some thought.

Because so many documents float around, something has to differentiate one from the other. Some firms use colored covers. For most, titles are supposed to tell the tale. Titles are never short, as in "Plaintiff's Memorandum of Law." I once saw one that took up two pages. Here's an example: "The Memorandum of Law of Plaintiff XYZ Corporation in Support of Its Motion for a Preliminary Injunction Restraining Defendant ARC Corporation from its Outrageous Theft of Trade Secrets and Employees of XYZ Corporation in Pursuit of ARC Corporation's Attempt to Monopolize and Monopolization of the Defined Market and Submarkets as Defined Herein." The defendant's memorandum of law will then cite it is in answer to plaintiff's memorandum, giving plaintiff's entire title, and then defendant's title in response.

Turn the page and you get the title all over again, and then a brief description in ten or twelve pages setting forth the history of the case, the facts, and what will be indisputably[1] proven in the memorandum. Then you get the Legal Analysis, broken up into Points, sub-points, sub-sub-points, and submarines. But the wording is always the same.

"Plaintiff will prove indisputably that this state has consistently held that a defendant may not bugger a corpse and, therefore, can be held liable for civil damages, including punitive damages. But in this instance, the facts and the law clearly show that not just the law, but equity favors plaintiff because of the utterly egregious nature of defendant's actions. As stated by Justice Cardozo in <u>X v. Y</u>, ### N.Y. ####, #### (19___): "Those who are necessitous shall never be stripped of their rights before the courts of law and equity, for society is immersed in those philosophical pursuits which make us human and, perhaps great. We shall not turn our backs on such efforts.""

Let's note now that in certain states, such as California and New York, there are only one or two judges who are acknowledged as great or great looking. In California, Traynor was great, and Rose Bird was great looking (good enough to become a news broadcaster after she was unseated); in New York, Cardozo was great. The quote given above is fictional, but the fact is Cardozo, although considered a God (people were known tò throw themselves at his feet), was not always particularly clear in his phraseology. Thus, the same quote often can be used by both plaintiff and defendant, and will then be cited by the court for a completely different proposition.

The Legal Analysis involves an introductory paragraph introducing the elements that plaintiff will indisputably prove, or that defendant can never prove. Thus,

"Defendant's contentions to the contrary notwithstanding[2] that no breach was ever committed flies in the face of the indisputable facts. And, as will be shown clearly herein, those facts meet the elements long established by the highest court in this state.

"The elements composing breach are as follow: 1) a contract came into existence; 2) defendant did not perform; 3) plaintiff sustained damages ...," and so on.

After that comes the string of cases. If there is one good, high court opinion, that will be dwelled upon with great length and detail much in the manner of a child holding up a shiny rock and gazing at the reflection of each facet in the sun. Those cases going against the opinion will be distinguished in a footnote or not mentioned at all. Other supporting cases will be mentioned in a "string cite," which is a paragraph of ten or so cases.

A glaring defect in many memoranda, particularly those from

POINT I

DEFENDANT'S CONTENTION THAT PLAINTIFF HAS NO
CAUSE OF ACTION IS SPECIOUS AND A MISSTATEMENT OF
THE FACTS AND THE LAW FOR AS PLAINTIFF INDISPUTA-
BLY SHOWS THE LAW OF THIS STATE HAS LONG ESTAB-
LISHED SUCH A CAUSE OF ACTION AND PLAINTIFF MEETS
EACH AND EVERY ELEMENT

A. Plaintiff has Indisputably Met Its Burden of Proof as to the Four
Elements of Breach.

The law of this state has always recognized the four [1]

----

1. Defendant spuriously argues that the number "four" does not
mean what it says. The contention is absurd and not worthwhile of note.
See A. Kosnowfsky, Construction of Numbers in the Law: A State by
State Analysis, at 196 (1978 and Supplement 1984). As Cardozo stated in
X v. Y, ### N.Y. ###, ### (19__):

"Mathematics is an exacting science. There would be no certainty to life,
indeed, if that which we acknowledge as being universal in import was, instead, merely a passing whim. To sail on a boat, to watch the sun rise, to
perpetuate the constructs of society and the political umbrella would lose
all tangible sensation were one to believe that that which is, is not."

Certainly, defendant's argument is nothing more than "a frog in the
empty pond." A v. B, ### F.2d ###, ### (2d Cir. 1976). Defendant's
attempt at frivolity is better suited to places other than the courtroom, especially considering the facts at hand. This result cannot be gainsaid.
Plaintiff has leant over backwards to give credence to defendant's ridicu-
lous contentions only because of the professional courtesy plaintiff feels
is due, but this sally cannot be ignored. As stated by Justice Holmes in R
v. S, ### F.2d ###, ### (2d Cir. 19__): "If we take the hypotenuse of
the claim and divide it by its tangent, then certainly the radius shall
appear, beyond doubt." So, too, here, four is only four and nothing more,
nor less.

(Footnote continued on next page)

major firms, is that cases are often misquoted or cited for a proposition they do not stand for. A misquote is where an argument leads up to a case as holding for a certain proposition and then quotes from that case a statement facially supporting the proposition -- because the author has deleted an important sentence or two that otherwise changes the entire meaning of the declaration.

A case is improperly cited where, as with many treatises, it is listed as supporting a proposition with which it has *nothing* to do.

In law school, the general form of bluffing a thought is taught as legal writing, but there is no consistency from firm to firm as to favored words or phrases. At one firm I worked at, the tendency was to use "In any event" in every third paragraph. Much to my chagrin, my next firm was quite adverse to "In any event" and, instead, preferred "to wit." My first session with the partner I was working for almost ended up in fisticuffs, since "to wit," pronounced rapidly enough, sounds like something else.

Because local court rules generally provide for limitations on the length of memoranda or briefs, those documents will tend to have a myriad of footnotes.

An appellate level brief or memorandum of law differs from the lower court memorandum in that briefs are graced with a table of contents and table of authorities.

In writing a brief or memorandum, the rule of thumb is that the highest court in the jurisdiction is the best authority (if it favors your case), then other courts in the jurisdiction, then cases from other states, then treatises, and then law journal articles. Treatises deserve special attention because they are cited to with some frequency. Apparently, no one bothers to check the cases the treatises cite to. I have yet to discover a treatise which properly states the law and cites to cases actually supporting that proposition.

By the way, memoranda are often submitted to a court along with supporting documents, such as affidavits. An affidavit is a document giving facts known to the affiant personally and is, of course, written by the attorney who has no personal knowledge of the facts and who wants or needs certain facts to fit his case. The affidavit, invariably written at the penultimate moment, is signed by

91

SELECTED WORDS AND PHRASES

For Briefs	For Advisory Memoranda
To wit	It seems
Gainsaid	It appears
Not to be denied	It could be
Notwithstanding	It might be
To the contrary notwithstanding	It should be
In any event	In any event
Heretofore	One might assume
Therefor, therefore	It could be assayed that
As pointed out in	Hopefully, if
Specious	Egregious
Irrelevant	Of relevance might be
Totally insupportable proposition	One might presume that

---

the affiant at the last moment.

Before leaving this topic of memoranda, the question arises as to what happens to all these papers? The memorandum, after all, is one of a set of documents. In a motion to dismiss or for summary judgment, we have had at least a complaint served. In a motion brought after issue has been joined, we may have had the complaint, the answer, a reply to counterclaims, discovery requests, discovery, depositions, and so on. In any event, the case will have accumulated a solid five hundred hours of billable time.

The answer is, I don't know what happens to all those pieces of paper, since they matter little in most cases, which are settled.

In-House Memoranda And Opinions

The genre of in-house memoranda is not limited to litigation associates but is, instead, the manna of all departments. This work is never shown to clients, but is instead an advisory letter to the partner who will then communicate his conclusions to the client. This work is, however, paid for by the client.

The in-house memorandum introduces us to the world of redundancy in format and phrasing. It is the memorandum that begins with a statement of the issue, facts, and conclusions, and then goes into a legal analysis, and then conclusions. Since it is used in-house, it is not written in the subjunctive, but the genetic associate knows that it is written in the alternative. The reason the genetic associate drafts an in-house memorandum in the alternative is because no lawyer wants to be pinned down in the event that someone actually relies on his advice.

As pointed out previously, many memoranda and briefs are merely copied from other memoranda and briefs. Many in-house memoranda written at major firms are basically plagiarized from treatises. And, as noted above, many treatises make up the law and cite to cases having nothing to do with those imaginary propositions.

Advisory opinions are written for the client and are infected with subjunctives and alternatives. They, too, have their statements of issues and facts and conclusions and conclusions, and are bound in thick paper and sometimes autographed. Advisory opinions always have words such as "Confidential," or "Attorney-Client Work Product" typed on them, because the attorney does not want any other attorney to get at the opinion during discovery for the sake of having a good laugh. Since lawyers do not advise clients on ultimate business decisions, the client is left to figure out what to do from the thousands of would's, could's, may's, and or's littering the memorandum.

A SAMPLE ADVISORY MEMORANDUM FOR A CLIENT

EYES ONLY
CONFIDENTIAL AND PRIVILEGED
ATTORNEY/CLIENT WORK PRODUCT
YOU CANNOT GET THIS DOCUMENT IN DISCOVERY
DO NOT READ

To: Vemmerfestzerlicher Enterprises
From: Alvin Chipmunk, Esquire
Dated: x/y/z

ADVISORY OPINION WITH REGARD TO LAXATIVES

FACTS

With increasing frequency, laxative companies such as Vemmerfestzerlicher Enterprises (hereinafter, "VE") have been issuing psyllium hydrophillic mucilloid laxatives for over-the-counter non-prescription drug and pharmaceutical sale incorporating the letters "l," "a," and "x" somewhere in the brand name.

The primary psyllium hydrophillic mucilloid laxative manufacturer, Kosnowfsky Drugs (hereinafter, "X"), uses the names Laxalax, Axalax, Havealax and Belugalax (hereinafter, the "X names"). All X names were registered as trademarks in 19___.

VE has begun selling a psyllium hydrophillic mucilloid laxative it calls Coronalax. The name has not been registered.

X is now threatening to file suit against VE on trademark infringement grounds, including pendent causes of action in unfair competition and related state claims. Although at least a dozen other manufacturers of psyllium hydrophillic mucilloid laxatives incorporate the letters "l," "a," and "x" somewhere in the brand name, some of them having done so for upwards of ten years, this threatened suit by X against VE would be its first against a psyllium hydrophillic mucilloid laxative manufacturer incorporating the letters "l," "a," and "x" somewhere in the brand name.

ISSUES

The primary issues are what sort of marks are herein involved; and whether laches and estoppel are valid defenses against the potential X claim.

CONCLUSIONS

(1) Although the factors used in trademark infringement cases are not always the same depending upon the whim of the judge, one might say that some of the primary, general factors are strength of the mark; actual confusion; marketing channels; proximity of the goods; similarity of the marks; type of goods; type of purchase; and defendant's intent.

Of the types of marks one might consider, the weakest is the generic mark. Generic marks are probably the weakest because they cannot be protected. A generic mark could be generic because it is, or because it has become generic, as by being listed in a dictionary as a generic word. Aspirin is probably one example here.

The strongest marks are suggestive, arbitrary or fanciful. They may be suggestive, arbitrary or fanciful because they have no direct relationship to the product. Giving the name "cola" to a rubber tire could be one example.

Marks that cannot be protected except with a showing of secondary meaning are descriptive marks. A descriptive mark could describe the product in some manner.

It could be argued that a psyllium hydrophillic mucilloid laxative -- and, by the way, psyllium hydrophillic mucilloid laxatives are made from the husks of the psyllium seed, Plantago ovata, as opposed to the dried bark of Rhamnus purshiana or the remains of Cassia acutifolia -- given a name containing the letters "l," "a," and "x," is descriptive because "lax" means a looseness or openness, which would seem to be the desired effect of swallowing a dose of psyllium seed husks.

[Another ten pages on this particular conclusion.]

(2) Laches is a defense apparently meaning that the plaintiff has inexcusably delayed. Estoppel seems to be a defense meaning that the plaintiff is estopped from pursuing a suit. It would seem here that, because X has never before claimed infringement against the other manufacturers of psyllium hydrophillic mucilloid laxatives using names including the letters "l," "a," and "x," and moreover since it seems that VE expended large sums of money in developing, naming and marketing its own psyllium hydrophillic mucilloid laxative using the letters "l," "a," and "x," that X would be estopped and lached from bringing or pursuing this claim.

[Another ten pages on this conclusion, followed by a Legal Analysis setting forth the facts, conclusions and law using headings, sub-headings and sub-sub-headings, topped off with another set of Conclusions. The Appendix will have a list of leading laxatives.]

Footnotes:

1. Indisputable, nondisputable, undisputable, and not to be disputed are the most frequently used words in memoranda. Only the first and the last examples are proper but, even so, overuse has lessened the value of stating that a proposition cannot be debated, especially in the context of a litigious flurry of pleadings that can survive a motion to dismiss only if a dispute is created.

2. "To the contrary notwithstanding" is another pet of the law. In olde English, notwithstanding is notwibstondynge, as derived from non obstant, the latter derived from obstino, meaning "to be resolved with regard to something." In opposition to a "contrary notwithstanding" is a "gainsaid," which is an archaic form of saying something cannot be denied because its nature is unquestionable.

CHAPTER FIVE

PARTNERS TRAIN ASSOCIATES?

From Racquet Ball To Divorce

Partners (and senior associates) are supposed to train new associates. This training involves proper research techniques; the writing of documents in accordance with the firm's style; how to look at an issue and perceive all the angles, no matter how arcane; and how to act in court, in conference, and with clients.

However, since partners have not done research in years, have never been in court, have not written a document since being promoted (becoming editors instead), and have relied on senior and junior associates to perceive the issues, about all a partner can teach an associate is how to tastefully order drinks and food and carry on an affair with a secretary.

Moreover, partners are deeply offended if a new associate reveals knowledge, non-legal abilities, or emotions of any sort. They want answers going directly to resolving an issue with the least amount of legal pain and the greatest number of billable hours. Knowledge, for example, means reading fiction, philosophy, or history and bringing it up by analogy. Genetic lawyers do not read anything outside of what is necessary to the practice.

A non-legal ability would be the ability to write. An associate has to readily adapt to accepting the fascination lawyers have with being redundant and dry. Worse is where an associate writes a trade book and has it published. The only exoneration would be to dedicate the book to the firm so that the firm receives free advertising. (I was once thanked profusely for remarrying and including a blurb on my then firm in the New York Times. Better than a match box.)

Oddly enough, there are non-legal abilities which are considered legal abilities depending upon the fashionable fad. One example is racquet ball. For a while, it was almost impossible to walk down the hallway of any firm without risking injury by being jabbed with the shafts of racquets.

Emotions are not permitted unless for an approved activity involving constitutional implications, such as anti-discrimination organizations or the ACLU. In those cases, emotions are acceptable as long as they are proved by contributing a portion of one's salary to the annual fundraising drive. The emotion is acceptable because a firm's total contribution is then ranked in law publications and it is important to be in the top ten for public relations' purposes.

Other emotions not resulting in favorable publicity are *verboten*. These include human emotions. One can assume with certainty that male partners seem to get a tremendous thrill from causing female associates to cry. I have seen and heard this story so many times, it is like watching reruns during the summer.

Another forbidden human emotion is love. If an associate is not married when he or she starts practice in a large firm, he or she will end up marrying, if at all, through something arranged by parents. Dates will invariably have to be broken because partners can always sense when an associate needs to see someone outside of the law; partners are always leaving at six o'clock to catch the train and they have hysterical smiles because the associate has been left behind to work through the night. The date has to be broken; after the second time, the other person won't even make the date.

Where an associate is already married (and remember from a previous chapter that many third year law students marry from the fear that they will be unable to meet anyone to marry once they start work), conjugal relations are frowned upon. From a legal standpoint, one might think this somewhat obtuse, since lawyers often include loss of consortium in lawsuits involving spouses. They weren't able to join, your honor, *members* of the jury, and damages must be awarded. That's fine in the courtroom but not in the legal bedroom.

The reasons are based upon a partner's own perception of what marriage is. It is something to have for weekend parties during which clients are entertained. Most partners see their wives (and children) during waking hours only on weekends. The wife must know how to dial caterers. The children must take tennis and racquet ball lessons. The wife must be attractive -- that is, she should dye her hair blond, wear blue-colored contact lenses, and show cleavage -- and she must be vacuous. She must never, never, upstage the partner during the Saturday night blow-out or the Sunday afternoon brunch during which neighbors are handed business cards. As if a Catholic, the partner will have sex with the wife only on Saturday night and that for the purpose of procreating future lawyers. The rest of the week, he has his secretary, or paralegal, or the female associate coming up for partnership in one or two years.

Following is a composite of a normal event occurring on a late weekday night. The partner and the associate are in the partner's office reviewing affidavits, memoranda, and discovery requests. On the large rosewood desk are jagged piles of papers, thousands of half-chewed pencils, a crumpled cellophane bag, and an open bag of potato chips.

The partner's phone rings. The conversation from his end sounds like this:

PARTNER: Oh. Hi, dear. Yes, I'm still at the office. You called me here, didn't you? No, I'm sorry, I didn't mean anything derogatory about that. So someone's banging on the front door, what do you expect me to do about it? You know I have to get these papers out. He's probably just drunk and forgot his keys and thinks our apartment is his. He tried raping you in the elevator and has a gun? Look, I don't know about that. I wasn't there. No, I'm not saying you're lying, but maybe you're overreacting. You know you exaggerate fact patterns. I have to get back to these papers. I'll call you in an hour or so.

The partner hangs up the phone, grabs a handful of chips, stuffs

101

those and a pencil eraser into his mouth, and returns to the papers. The phone rings.

PARTNER [*grumbling*]: Where's the damned night-time receptionist?

ASSOCIATE [*mumbling tensely*]: It's after eleven.

The partner picks up the phone.

PARTNER: Yes. Yes, I'm still here. All right, you called the doorman and he isn't there. I know, I can hear the baby crying in the background. It is hard to get through on the police emergency number. I'll be back in a few hours. Why don't you just calm down and take care of the baby? He probably needs his diapers changed. I have to get back to my papers.

He slams down the receiver, holds the bag of chips over his mouth, empties it, chews, taps a pencil between his teeth, picks up the greasy papers, glares at the phone, listens to it ring, glares at the associate, then picks up the receiver.

PARTNER: He what? He broke a hole in the door? Do you realize how expensive doors are? How could you let him do that? Shit, now I have to buy a new door. I can't believe this. And these papers are due Monday. What's the matter with you? Hello? Hello?

Emotions by definition do not include being upset over a divorce. A divorce is an objective, legal machination. An associate undergoing a divorce should be excited by the prospect of getting to the jugular of the ex-spouse. Firms will even list the divorces of associates (and partners) as nonbill matters, which means that the services of the firm can be used although the work performed will not be counted toward one's billable (and therefore valuable) hours.

Children are in the same boat. If the divorce involves children, the implication is that the associate should not seek custody. Children represent something of a dilemma because it is hard to condemn the time and care they require. A wife or ex-wife can always fend for herself. Unless the associate promises to hire an *au pair* (a young European female, usually French, who comes to the States to take care of children and hopefully marry an American, but in the meantime providing sexual pleasure to all concerned) or a South American maid, it will be suggested that he yield custody on two grounds having nothing to do with love: 1) the child will eventually love the associate more in the future; and 2) the rule of law (regardless of what the law itself says) is that the woman will get custody anyway.

The female associate who gives birth is also frowned upon, particularly if she opts to breast-feed. Years ago, Western Electric (pre-AT&T-divestiture) instituted a part-time program for its female lawyers. As I recall, they could work two and half to three day weeks, retaining benefits. A few years after that, some of the law firms declared that they would be formulating plans for their pregnant associates. The first plan that evolved went something like this: The associate would get two months off after birth without pay; the associate would then have to return to work and work a minimum forty hour week; the associate would be paid one half of her class's going salary; and the associate would have to contribute to benefits. The associate would not be in the firm's pension plan. Since then, firms have experimented with maternity and paternity leave, and part-time lawyering. But in all events, associates here will lose out due to disproportionately lower salaries or lack of benefits; increased drudge work, similar to being a paralegal; the knowledge that you are off partnership track (or that you will be put back a year or two); and heightened emotional irresponsibility, in that loving parents often exhibit distractions due to worry about one's child.

Morality

But the worse emotion is wavering on an issue because the opposing side seems to be *right*. The most demoralizing situation is where the law is clear, but the morality of the case is dehumanizing.

Philosophy of the law is a subject taught in many of the top schools. The topic is one that intrigued every European theologian, philosopher, logician, and mathematician until this country won its independence from Britain. Since then, we have separated morality from the law for two reasons: 1) our laws must be subjectively objective (that is, whoever is in power gets to write laws, and whoever is sitting on the bench gets to analyze those laws); and 2) our laws must be dissociated from religious or minority persuasions.

There have been and are some American philosophers of the law -- Marcuse and Dworkin come to mind -- but the association of law with anything outside of itself has become *passe* unless one is attempting to cram one's own beliefs down everyone else's throats. Although we might speak of morality or equate that with the Word of God (as interpreted by us, having had multiple visions during a long weekend in Taos), all we are really talking about is the power of pushing legislators or judges up for reelection into adopting our narrow points of view. The Meese report on pornography and its tremendous moral impact on having *Playboy* removed from 7-Eleven stores is a fine example of morality triumphing over the Constitution and common sense; another involves religious fanatics who bomb abortion clinics because it is more moral to kill pregnant women than to permit pregnant women to have an abortion.

So we don't really have a philosophy of law; we have certain socio-political-theological-economic concerns that are lobbying or bombing to get rid of horrible things like genitals, breasts, freedom of choice, and privacy behind closed doors.

Since the above are wonderful ways to generate legal fees, lawyers do not look into the true moral concerns behind the idiocies involved in groups attempting to force themselves on the rest of us regardless of consequences. As long as there is some statutory or decisional writing (or loophole), it is sufficient that the client pays.

To return to the most offensive exhibition of emotion in a law firm, consider the case of a non-English speaking family trying to make it in America. When you practice law for a large firm, your client will be the bank, not the poor family. The papers you see will merely state that the defendants or the bankrupt persons owe money to the bank on a note and that the bank has a legal right to foreclose. It is not until you go to court in the middle of winter carrying your ironclad, irrefutable motion papers that you will see not only the family which lives in the cramped house in a bad neighborhood, but also whom they have been able to afford as their attorney. There will be five sickly but beautiful children. The wife will be obese but working twenty hours a day at two jobs netting $2.75 an hour. The husband will have been a trained carpenter, currently out of work due to union troubles and because he fell from a building and hurt his back. He does not have medical insurance or the money necessary for treatment. The attorney will be a harried associate from an unranked law school grossing $15,000 a year from a partner who has dreams of creating the next Jacoby & Meyers. The attorney will have three litigation bags overflowing with cases and he or she will have little knowledge of the matter at hand.

Since the bank can pay, your papers will have been drawn up by you, a junior associate, a senior associate, and at least one partner. Research will have been extensive. The judge knows the lead partner on the case and also knows that when he leaves the bench, he must keep his options open with regard to which firm he will join (more on this in the chapter on judges).

You observe the family; you watch the snow falling; you listen to the absurd, stuttering argument of their attorney; you glance at your file of papers, case listings, photographs, and exhibits. You hear the judge telling the attorney how off the wall he or she is and how he's had it with firms that advertise in match books and subways. And you know as you rise for your argument that you will win and that this family, having absolutely no idea as to what is going on, will be out on the street in the middle of winter.

Can you do anything for this family? Of course not; you have no right to try to reach a settlement, for this is only one of a thousand similar cases the bank, the firm's client, has on hand. The bank doesn't want to be bothered. The law firm doesn't want to be bothered. You have to shut your eyes and give your statement and listen to the judge patting you and the firm on the back and you have to see through the family as it trudges out of the courthouse still not knowing what has occurred since their attorney does not speak Spanish.

Even worse can happen in organizations such as Legal Aid. These associations contract with local governments to defend people indicted on criminal charges. In the vast majority of cases, the "clients" are not only admittedly guilty of the charges, but also have a string of priors (previous convictions). In many cases, the clients are in jail and will send postcards or letters to assigned female attorneys saying things like: I am sure that you are very attractive and will get me out of jail and then I would like to meet with you I have looked up your address in the New York Law Journal since it was printed when you passed the bar exam. I am six foot seven inches and weigh three hundred pounds and have been weight lifting.

Almost all of these cases are defended on purely procedural grounds. And half the time, an appellate court will bend over backwards to approve of a retrial or dismissal, in great part because of competition with appellate courts in neighboring districts which have come out with opposing decisions (this having to do with possible appointments to the next higher appellate level). This area of law is therefore devoted to a grasping at straws syndrome: the organization defending the indicted and imprisoned will toss canned briefs at the courts in the hope that one objection will work for whatever judicial reason. What the client has done is dissociated from supposedly objective analyses involving procedures; what the client is capable of doing is tossed aside. If you object and say that there really is no ground for appeal, you will find yourself walking the streets (possibly with the client). Unlike civil law, where frivolous suits are finally being frowned upon, criminal law promotes frivolity. Appeals are its *sine qua non*. But are those appeals necessary for the rights of the client (let one real criminal go free so that the innocent will be served), or because these organizations of lawyers need to

WAYS OF TRAINING ASSOCIATES

Assign no work every other week, making the associate believe his work is not up to snuff.

On late Friday afternoons, assign SEC filings, answers to temporary restraining orders, or other matters requiring an immediate response on Monday (which matters have been on the partner's desk for a month).

Mark up every document handed in by an associate with illegible comments, emphasized with exclamation points. Illegible notations are accomplished using a stencil available from Blumberg Forms.

Have two associates research the same issue, then have them come to the office so that they can be asked why they found different cases.

Have the female associate water plants, get coffee, and test the temperature of food.

Send a new associate to court to handle an oral motion without telling the associate anything about the issues or court procedure.

Bring an associate onto a matter with which the firm has been struggling for ten years without getting anywhere and, at the first meeting with ten partners and twenty senior associates in attendance, ask the associate for his opinion.

In the old days, the quickest way to deplete an associate was to assign an antitrust case involving AT&T or IBM. Ah well, there must be some other case brewing involving four hundred thousand pounds of discovery documents.

Have the female associate sit on the most uncomfortable chair so that she will have to keep shifting her legs.

Put a plodding, stable male associate into a small room with a ravishing, underdressed female associate who is always leaving to attend to partners while insisting that the male associate take phone messages for her, which are unending.

Assign a sharp associate in a large firm matters never involving more than $500 in claims.

show their value to the local government when contracts come up for renewal, and the best way to show value is by declaring that a hundred thousand appeals were filed in the previous year?

The system itself can now proclaim with satisfaction that there have been attempts in recent years to cut down on lawsuits aimed solely at harassing others. But those sanctions for "frivolous" civil suits ignore the moral reality and at most give a wrist-slap to those who can afford a violent and prolonged spanking. For example, in the case of *Warner Bros. Inc. v. Dae Rim Trading Inc. and Yun Yon Cho*, plaintiffs (the name to the left of the *v.*) filed a copyright infringement suit in 1984 in the Southern District of New York (a federal court). The suit was based on the film, *Gremlins*, and one of its ancillary rights -- spinoff merchandising. In 1984, the film had grossed over $142 million, and merchandising had added another $8.4 million.

The defendants (listed to the right of the *v.*) were a bunch of non-English speaking Koreans who supplied goods to street peddlers and flea markets. They worked longer hours than a first year litigation associate at a major firm and probably made about a thousand times less per year. They had a handful of unlicensed Gremlin dolls for sale.

On the law, plaintiffs were *right*. That is, they had a legal right to sue anyone selling an unlicensed good derived from the copyrighted film. But look at how they used that right: even though they had already purchased six of the infringing dolls, they nonetheless had a judge sign an *ex parte* temporary restraining order (ex parte means without a hearing or notice to the defendants) permitting a search of the entire store; one of plaintiffs' attorneys had the wife of the store owner sign a consent to an injunction prohibiting future sales (even though the wife could barely speak English and had no lawyer); and they pressed the suit for three years.

Legal rights are supposed to lead to legal remedies. In this case, plaintiffs could not prove actual damages and so ended up with minimum statutory damages of a hundred bucks (and, presumably, a permanent injunction against the future sale of the unlicensed goods, which is something they could have settled for three years before). But the copyright act also provides that the prevailing party can receive attorney's fees, and plaintiffs asked for about $166,000. The judge at this point said, Enough is enough.[1]

In that case, it was the associate who apparently did most of the dirty work, such as getting the wife to sign the consent. What happens when an associate objects? He is fired. In a matter involving the "morality" established by the professional code of ethics, a senior partner and an associate were disqualified from handling a case for defendants when they (allegedly) improperly contacted plaintiff-corporation to discuss facts material to the case.

The associate claimed that he had nothing to do with the unethical behavior, but that the partner and law firm ignored his requests that he be permitted to exonerate himself. Instead, he was suddenly "escorted" from his office and, presumably, dumped onto the street.[2]

In other words, there is a confusion of legal rights, remedies, sanctions, and ethics that will never be sorted out until the kingpin of the law is brought to bear: money. Partners always become extremely agitated when associates waffle an issue because the other side is legally or morally right and, obviously, an associate who does not go along and convince himself that it is his job to be an adversary (that is, destroy the other side) is soon out-the-door. But partners will always pause and cock their heads if the wind carries the message that they might not receive their fees. In the Warner Brothers case, the law firm undoubtedly received its $166,000; in the matter involving the fired associate, the disqualified partner undoubtedly received his fees (and perhaps a pat on the back from the client for being so devious).

The only time I have seen partners sweat was when a federal law was enacted permitting the government to "trace" illegally received assets, such as money coming in from drug trafficking, and to put a clamp on them until the case was resolved. The impact was directed against criminal lawyers defending drug honchos, because the money could be traced even unto the hallowed domain of the lawyer's bank account. Suddenly, the issue of defending known drug dealers to the hilt had a second thought to it.

THE MAJOR ISSUES RAISED IN EVALUATIONS

How Partner X doesn't like your work, although you never did work for Partner X and don't even know who he is.

How Partner Y observed that you were never in your office available for assignments, although you were always in the library doing research for him.

How you did not order a martini during a business lunch. Since you were the one first asked to order, no one else could order a martini and only white wine spritzers were served.

How you (a female associate) showed a rebellious attitude against tradition by not participating in the wet T-shirt contest during the firm's summer outing.

How your emotions are uncontrolled and unsuitable for the practice of law because you: 1) cried over your divorce or loss of child custody; 2) left work early two days in a row because your child was sick; 3) objected to contributing fifty or more dollars to the sole organization supported by the firm, announcing instead that you were giving a large donation to public radio; 4) wrote and directed a skit at the firm outing which realistically spoofed the partners; 5) tried dating.

And the second thought was resolved with a shake of the head. The solution has become this: have the client pay a large retainer in cash.

Evaluations

Associates are supposed to be "evaluated" once or twice a year by the partner or partners who directly supervise their growth as lawyers. Associates are also supposed to receive on-the-spot comments from all partners and senior associates with regard to their daily projects and general appearance.

Utter silence is one technique that partners have developed, since it can be construed as either condemnation or praise. By utter silence is meant a silence so intense, so devoid of a sense of life, that its decibel level (0) is used to calibrate the "dead rooms" of research labs.

Silence can also be used at the firm cocktail parties or outings, as in an associate standing or sitting alone. If, for example, you are invited to a firm outing with your spouse, and find that the two of you are seated at an otherwise empty table, it is suggested that you apply for a job as a train conductor.

Sometimes, a partner will break utter silence. One way is for the partner to stare at the wall or ceiling for ten or fifteen minutes and then suddenly sigh.

Another way is for the partner to suddenly start davaning before letting out a groan more horrifying than anything on the soundtrack of *Aliens*.

Other ways of abruptly ending silence are to break a pencil; eat a mouthful of potato chips; rub shoes together; hum; smack lips; crack knuckles; bang spoons against one's cuffs.

The point is to test the mettle of the associate while suggesting he could be off partnership track. A secondary object is to test the health of the associate's heart, particularly when utter silence is suddenly broken.

Silence is probably better than evaluations. One miserable day you are called into Partner X's office. On the way, you automatically pick up a legal pad and a handful of pencils, while wondering whether you have time to go to the bathroom. Partner X is behind his rosewood desk, on which is stacked everything you've ever researched, written, or thought. Partner Y sits on the gray wool couch. You must immediately decide whether to sit next to Y (whose arm is across the back of the open cushion), or on one of the two client chairs. You sit on a chair, which means you have to twist back and forth depending on which partner is talking.

111

PARTNER Y: I have one comment. I did not like that memo you did on the ABC case. It was a terrible memo.

ASSOCIATE: What memo for the ABC case?

PARTNER Y: The one involving, I don't really remember now, but I do remember I thought it was a shoddy piece of work.

ASSOCIATE: But the ABC case was before my time.

PARTNER Y: No. You definitely did that memo in the ABC case. I remember spending evenings here with you. You didn't grasp the issue at all.

ASSOCIATE: I swear, I wasn't here during the ABC case.

PARTNER X: Yes, I think he's right. I believe you're thinking of Associate R. Associate R was the associate who left just before he came on board. [*Note*: associates are always coming on board, even where a firm doesn't do any admiralty work.]

PARTNER Y: That's wrong. That's definitely wrong. Then maybe he worked on the memo with Associate R.

ASSOCIATE: But Associate R jumped ship before I came on board.

PARTNER X: That's right. Associate R had jumped ship.

The evaluation will go on for another hour, at the end of which Partner X will comment that the associate is right on track while Partner Y concludes that the associate is off track because of a memo he or she had not done in a matter that had closed months before the associate arrived at the firm. The illusory memo will thereafter come up at every evaluation.

Evaluations will inevitably end up concentrating on the smallest aspect of the associate's devoted life to the firm. Forget the 3,000 billed hours, the important point is that the associate could not fit a partner's last minute footnote into an already printed and bound brief due at court in an hour.

Another major stumbling block to making it in a firm that often comes up in evaluations is clothing. The senior associate who, for the first time in six years, is observed with the top button of his shirt unfastened because the air conditioning has broken down and the windows cannot be opened. The first year associate who is so indebted that he cannot afford new suits, ties, or shoes. The female associate who wears pants to work and then wears a skirt that is not hemmed over the knees (well over the knees). The associate who does not have his monogram on every piece of clothing when everyone else in the office has monograms.

The above examples, of course, are not to be confused with the associate bursting into the cocktail party with his tie undone and his shirt sleeves rolled up, for in that context, appearance is an expression of overwork and not of lack of etiquette. Clients, although billed for it, are not invited to cocktail parties.

The worse evaluation situation is where you know some of your work was shoddy but the shoddiness was caused by the partner. Only genetic lawyers can bluff through any task. The rest are left with the reality of assignments, and assignments are often incomplete or twisted. Consider the following hypothetical scenario.

PARTNER X: I would like you to write a brief memo on the following. Where Client A is a general depositor at a bank and the bank uses A's general deposit funds to purchase investment papers for the purpose of generating interest for A's deposit account, does the bank still retain the right of set off as against those funds? You don't have to see any of the documents. And don't worry about the facts. Just a quick memo. Nothing major.

The associate toddles off and does the short memo as requested.

For those who don't know what the above assignment is talking about, a bank has a right to set off monies in a general deposit against an indebtedness of the depositor which is due and owing to the bank. As opposed to a general deposit, a special deposit, arising either by contract or a course of conduct between the parties, is not subject to set off, since special deposits are earmarked for identified purposes, such as payroll.

In any event, the partner reads the draft memo, states that it is acceptable but would the associate try and get a better case or two. The associate does that and hands in the memo. There is no feedback from the partner.

Not until evaluation time, that is, and that can be six months or a year down the road. Then the scene is this. The partner is sitting on a chair with his legs crossed. The upper leg is swinging nervously back and forth. A dark cloud hugs the partner's face. He is frowning. On his lap is a stack of memoranda. The associate sits on the couch, clutching his yellow legal pad to his chest. The air is thick with accusation.

The first memo the partner pulls from his pile is the set off memo. He waves it in the air.

PARTNER X: Look at this. I have never seen work like this in my life. You did not follow the proper style, you have the issue completely wrong, the research stinks, and you left out all the facts and didn't even have the decency to cite to any of the documents. The documents were the essence of this project. I have shown this memo to everyone else in the firm and everyone agrees that it is the worse memo they have ever read.

ASSOCIATE: I don't understand. That's the memo you approved. And you said not to worry about the facts or look at the documents.

PARTNER X: You are missing my point. That is the whole problem with you. You are always missing my point. God, why do I get all the losers? Look at the issue alone. Bank, set off, general deposit, investment papers. That's completely wrong. The issue is: Where a non-depositor asks a bank to act as agent for the purchase of investment papers, does the bank have a right of set off?

ASSOCIATE: But that issue has nothing to do with the issue in the memo.

PARTNER X: You agree with me. See? Even you agree with me. I'll tell you one thing. You're not working for me again. And I'll see to it that you don't work with anyone else in this firm. That's all.

If you think that is bad, the truth is evaluations have little to do with the evaluation process. As the genetic lawyer knows, the real evaluations are the day-to-day back slappings, lunches, dirty jokes, and drinking, and how those are translated at Professional Development Committee meetings. It is at those meetings, where partners sit around a conference table and eat croissants with strawberry jam, that a partner will say what he wants other partners to believe about a certain associate.

If, over a seven year period, the partner says, "This guy is just wonderful. The firm couldn't get along without him," the odds are the associate will make partner unless the associate inadvertently drops his pants at the last minute. But if the partner keeps saying, "You know, this guy is not doing the work. I'd like to call some headhunters and see about replacing him," then that associate's days are numbered.

Of course, at an evaluation meeting with that associate, the same partner could very well be saying, "Your work is top notch." This is part of the game, which is sometimes played out with the content associate sitting in his office one morning and the door suddenly opening. In the doorway are the recruiter and a new face.

The recruiter says to the associate, "I wanted you to meet Associate R, who is beginning work here today." Associate R smiles and holds out his hand. "Hi. Sorry to hear about you leaving. Since

What You Aren't Supposed To Know ...

I'm getting your office anyway, could you leave your form files in the drawers? It would make it so much easier."

Footnotes:

1. The judge also noted, "I find that Spielberg was a dominant voice in copyright enforcement, if not the dominant voice." So goes the E.T. philosophy.
2. Shaun Assael, "Phillips, Nizer Ex-Associate Says He Was Fired Unjustly," Manhattan Lawyer, Nov. 17 - Nov. 23, 1987, p. 4.

CHAPTER SIX

SUPPORT STAFF

The ratio of associates to partners can range from one to one at a small firm, to six or more to one at a large firm. The ratio of support staff to lawyers can be even higher.

Support staff forms a society separate from lawyers. Except for giving orders or having sex, lawyers are not supposed to socialize with this second world.

Support staff can be divided into paralegals; secretaries; receptionist; word processing pool; librarian and assistants; managing clerk; administrative chief; general administration (messengers, copiers, mail room); and the whorehouse.

Paralegals

Until 1983, paralegals were what the name implied: people without law degrees who had taken courses in helping out lawyers. In general, paralegals are supposed to perform directed legal research (that is, look up and shepardize cases and statutes pursuant to a narrow list drawn up by the attorney); maintain files of forms (the backbone of the practice of law); create and update lists of documents for each matter; fill out and file forms; and water plants.

Paralegals used to be kept in pools until it was discovered that they tended to wrinkle. Thereafter, they were permitted to join departments in the firm and specialize just like real lawyers.

The change that occurred in the early 1980's was that paralegals began cropping up who held valid law degrees. A lawyer working for one quarter or less of the going rate for real lawyers who get to give orders and drink Absolut? Instead of starting their own firm, working for a sole practitioner, or joining Jacoby & Meyers in a shopping

117

mall?

These paralegals fall into definable groups. The largest consists of graduates of unranked schools, most of whom have not passed the bar exam. They seem to feel that by working in a prestigious firm as a paralegal, some of that prestige will rub off on them so that when they pass the bar (which they generally never do), either the firm will up them to being associates (which the firms never do), or they will be able to move to a less prestigious firm (which they won't want to do when the time comes, unwilling to give up the polished wood, winding staircases, and glamour of the large firm).

Another group is composed of those associates who refuse to devote themselves around the clock to the practice of law because they have children at home. Only slowly does it dawn on them that paralegals are as mistreated as junior associates and that they too will be called upon to work nights and weekends.

A third group is those who did not make partner, of associate counsel, or eternal senior associate. Since they did not die or disappear (see the chapter on making partner), and since they were able to persuade the administrative chief (not the partners) that if they did not retain some sort of job with an income they and their babies would starve and their condo would be foreclosed upon, they have accepted the life of being laughed at.

Even law firms need their jokers, much like European courts during the reign of kings.

What do paralegals really do? First, they practice being depressed much of the time. Second, the good ones actually prop up their assigned attorneys by handling matters with a proficiency impossible to a lawyer.

Discounting lunches, dinners, parties, retreats, conferences, joke telling, and long distance telephone calls, the practice of law consists of paper pushing. For every document generated, a dozen other documents have to be filled out, filed, indexed, bound, mailed, or faxed. It is the paralegal who does the latter. It is the paralegal who has the forms, such as those for filing security interests, copyrights, and trademarks. It is the paralegal who knows how to fill out the forms, how much it costs to file them, and where to file them. If left to the attorney, the procedure of filling out and filing a simple form would entail two months' worth of legal research.

It is the paralegal who knows what the inside of the courthouse looks like. She can go there without turning green and actually retrieve documents, xerox them, and return to the firm without having a nervous breakdown. It is the paralegal who knows where the discovery documents are and what they say (although she will never be asked about their contents). It is the paralegal who knows that in another file for a different matter lies all of the xeroxed cases the partner is currently asking for, and she will save two days by having the xeroxes re-xeroxed.

In short, the paralegal often realizes that he or she is the one practicing most of the law, and that lawyers, left to their own devices, will inevitably screw things up.

Secretaries

Lawyers spend a great deal of time discussing, running after, hiring, firing, and training secretaries. At times, it seems that secretaries are the only inhabitants on earth other than lawyers (but then, lawyers are not really inhabitants; they are visiting earth prior to taking their seats on the right hand of God).

First, second, and third year associates, of course, have no say with regard to secretaries. They share secretaries with partners, which means they have no secretary. But junior and senior associates usually get to choose whom they want.

Although a nonbill, pro bono matter, associates and partners devote more energy to selecting a secretary than to any legal matter. Those slit skirts, see-through blouses, frilly bras, the boots, the calves, stockings, perfumes, smiles, the capped teeth, the coifed hair, the circus rouge, glistening lipstick, pink of the tongue, the total inability to take dictation or type. It is the secretaries who provide the adrenalin flow necessary for staying awake after a four martini lunch. It is the secretaries at the Christmas party who get drunk and let you fondle and kiss them. It is the secretaries who have to stay as

119

late as you do and then join you for a drink at a disco across the street. It is the secretaries who read romance novels and watch films starring Richard Gere who have dreams of bedding and wedding a lawyer and living happily ever after. It is the secretaries who do bed the lawyers and sometimes even have children and realize suddenly that it would be quite impossible for them to hire a lawyer from a match box or subway poster and win against a member of a five hundred lawyer firm.

But sometimes there is a last laugh for the young, attractive secretary. And a good laugh for the rest of the firm. I recall one time that a senior associate spent months interviewing until he selected a decidedly attractive young woman. Everyone would gather in the hallway to watch her pass. She was astonishing and amenable. She started going out with the associate after work. She and her associate would dance the night away. Then, after her first month had passed, she appeared one day with huge, open herpes sores on her mouth.

What associates begin to realize is that the young, attractive secretaries are not the ones they need. Outside of sex, the primary function of a secretary is to handle the lawyer's personal life. Secretaries keep the rolodex files of names, addresses, phone numbers; the dates for birthdays, anniversaries, and holidays; they order flowers sent, pay credit card bills, arrange vacations, calm down distraught spouses with lies, and get gossip from the major client's secretary.

Where paralegals keep the practice of law moving along, secretaries keep the lawyers moving along. Remove a partner's long-term secretary and he will flounder and finally topple over with a purple face. He will not know who he is, when he was born, who he is married to, whether he has children and, if he does, where they are. He will not know if he owes money to anyone, has one or two mistresses, or in which department he belongs. He will not know where his clothes are being dry cleaned, which restaurants and foods he prefers, or how his hair should be cut.

In other words, after the stint with the beautiful, incapable secretary, lawyers will opt for mom.

Receptionist

Since it is soon discovered that secretaries cannot be both beautiful and functional, the legal mind turns to hiring the stunning receptionist.

A receptionist has one task: to sit in the waiting room and make clients drool.

A top-notch receptionist will have been a dancer on the unexpurgated *Benny Hill Show*. She will be five feet eight inches tall. She will be blond and blue-eyed with a voice that melts honey. Her clothing, if existent, will consist of miniskirts with four slits; halter tops; and no underwear. Her face will compete with the covers of *Vogue* or *Cosmopolitan* (not *Interview*). The combination of her perfume and animal odors will so infect the waiting room that by the time clients are called in for the conference, they will have forgotten the matter to be discussed and will promptly pay any overdue bills.

It is sometimes said that a lawyer's primary consideration in moving from firm to firm is the receptionist. She is the ideal. She is someone who would have knocked the socks off Botticelli (if he had worn socks). She is someone who merely sits, her legs demurely crossed, and her sensuality bursting forth like a nova, almost too bright to be comprehended.

Word Processors

Law firms have been slow to computerize and, when they do, they frequently purchase the worse system at the highest price with the lousiest contract. Since the computerization is used essentially for word processing, temporary agencies, freelancers, and non-legal secretaries are in a good position to clean up.

As pointed out above, secretaries to the stars take care of lives. They are thus classified as legal secretaries and as such do little typing, and that on an IBM Selectric. Most legal documents are generated by the junior associates and it is they who must ensure that a document finds its way through the word processing center.

In large firms, the computers -- either a group of microcomputers or terminals connected to a minicomputer -- are usually located in some central office. Two mastiffs guard the entrance and, if you make it past them, the assistant administrator intercepts you. She is usually called Battle Ax and often carries one.

Since everyone knows that arbitrary, impossible deadlines are set on every matter a junior associate must accomplish, and since most of those deadlines are for the production of documents, the mastiffs, the Battle Ax, and the word processors are quite aware that they can make lawyers squirm, give them ulcers, and cause intestinal distress. Lawyers can always be seen pleading, kneeling, howling, and sobbing in the word processing center. And when you finally get Battle Ax to accept a document with a vague promise on when it will be ready for pick-up, a partner will walk in with a sheaf of personal correspondence which is, of course, given priority, bumping the work of associates down the ladder.

But let's say the document is accepted. There is no assurance that it will be done before the deadline and there is no guarantee that it will be done in the English language with appropriate structuring, such as tabs, spaces between words, and quotation marks. Battle Ax will always complain that the associate's handwriting is illegible, which may be true. Another explanation is that many of the day people just are not trained to use the equipment.

The problem is that people unfamiliar with computers will hire someone who says she is a word processor, whereas there is no such thing as a word processor. There are dozens of word processing programs on the market, and there are half a dozen operating systems, and now there are typesetting programs, and there are different types of printers -- and none of these elements seem to be taken into consideration.

A prime example of how mix-ups can occur involves some of the temp agencies. They advertise "Word Processors." Call them and ask for one and someone sweet and perhaps religious will be sent over. She will primly sit at the computer and say, "What now?" A more acute administrator might say, "Send me someone trained in Microsoft Word, Aldus Pagemaker/PC, and DOS 3.3." The agency will say, "Sure, we've got someone who can fit the bill," and they will send over someone sweet and perhaps religious who will sit at the computer and say, "What now?"

Even for in-house staff, little if any training is given. The impression seems to be that having bought a computer system, the system should train its users. So after all those hours of pleading, the returned document is utterly askew and unusable.

Often, it is the nighttime freelance staff which knows how to fly through the system. In Los Angeles and New York, these people tend to be actresses and actors who have discovered that specializing in word processing can be much more lucrative and less tiring than working as waitresses and waiters. They also get a kick out of making more per hour than the lawyers and they love the fact that the lawyers have to treat them with tremendous respect because otherwise they can move on to the next firm. Good word processors are in demand.

One sub-group involves proofreaders. Proofreaders live in a small room, sitting at a small round table, on which is a variety of dictionaries and cite books. Dictionaries are for checking spelling (because no one at the firm has figured out yet that word processors have automatic spell checkers and that even law dictionaries are available on diskette); cite books (also available on diskette for exorbitant amounts of money) are for ensuring that cases, statutes, and treatises are referred to in the proper manner.

When a proofreader first joins a firm, he will studiously mark up documents with questionmarks and suggestions as to grammar and content. After being yelled at by the lawyers and administrator, he will settle down to laughing softly and shaking his head while permitting one nonsensical brief after another to pass through his hands and, if he is lucky, out of mind.

Librarian

Librarians are the best law researchers in the business. After all, they buy the books and periodicals, and they peruse them as they come in. They are experts in doing computerized law searches. And they know the librarians at the other firms and bar associations, so they have a vast resource of knowledge to tap, and rare books that can be borrowed.

Librarians are also the only people in a law firm who know how to be administrators. The library is often given the least thought by lawyers with regard to space, demands made on it, or budget. While partners squabble over who gets the ever larger room with the rosewood furniture, the librarian must struggle with what he has. Late at night, one can often hear frazzled librarians walking hallways mumbling about shelf space.

While partners can readily ignore the library and its head, associates are at the mercy of the librarian and his staff. Since librarians know everything that is coming in, they can have selected copies made and routed to associates interested in or working on those topics. Being on a list is extremely important since associates, being overworked, can often neglect advance sheets (publications of cases prior to their going into bound books), or law journal articles.

Additionally, since librarians know where everything is located, they can find a book for an associate, whether in the firm's library or another's.

Although librarians are better trained than lawyers, they are not at all like lawyers. They tend to read outside of the law. For this reason, it is usually not the genetic lawyer, who will become partner, who befriends the librarian and learns the value of having someone erudite routing important materials to him or her. After all, each department purchases multiple copies of what they consider important publications, and the paralegals will send these originals to each associate.

It is the non-genetic lawyer who can discuss Dickens, Joyce, and parapsychology who will end up being the friend of the librarian. And, after that lawyer has left the firm, it will be the librarian he misses.

Managing Clerk

The managing clerk is the person who reports to the litigation department. She has her own staff for serving and filing papers. He or she compiles a weekly list of filing dates, hearings, trials, and appeals. This list is sent out to all lawyers in the firm as a public relations device, showing the other departments that the litigators are indeed producing income while prosecuting the world.

Nowadays, one can often find a paralegal serving as a managing clerk in departments such as real estate, corporations, and bankruptcy. Lists of closings, foreclosures, mergers, SEC filings, and creditors' committee meetings are circulated to the other departments to assure them that money is being made and fame procured.

Administrator

Office administrators are generally unapproachable by associates. They run around at the beck and call of partners, who love to scream at them as if the administrator, following through on one idiotic resolution or another recently passed by the lawyer's subcommittee on interior design, were responsible for the hallways being painted violet. Other than getting gray hair and ulcers, the only other task of an office administrator is to maintain a cash box full of hundred dollar bills for the use of the partners.

Remaining Staff

Remaining in-house staff include messengers; mailroom boys; copiers; staplers; and half a dozen gorgeous women whose job is to walk up and down hallways wearing stiletto heels. Everyone else wears blue cotton jackets so that it often seems that the firm is preparing to open a restaurant.

Relationship of Associates and Support Staff

To get anything done, a lawyer has two choices: become friendly with support staff; or abuse the staff into doing work.

Genetic associates and partners do the latter.[1] Other associates hobnob and therefore do not make partner.

After all, this staff, numbering in the hundreds, is a cross-section of humanity, living at the poverty level for messengers and at an unmarriageable age for the legal secretaries. They have problems and feelings. Aunts might need money for surgery; banks might be threatening to sue because payments were not timely made on a loan; they might feel their lives were ruined because of promises made and forgotten by a partner.

In short, they have the kinds of problems lawyers can handle. One call to the bank to arrange for an extended payment schedule; another call to a medical insurance company to discuss coverage; a suit filed against the partner.

But one cannot do that. It would not even be given nonbillable status. These matters mean nothing compared to the pro bono work being done defending the partner from the dog bite case.

The most one can do is to listen and give advice. In exchange, supplies are readily delivered, copies rapidly made, and friendships developed. But these are the real people of the world, and they don't have money or run corporations, so if an associate is seen too frequently smiling or laughing with the support staff, he develops a stigma which all the statutes in the world will not wash away.

Whorehouses

Law firms do use outside services with some frequency. A major service is the typesetting/print house, which prints up litigation backs and briefs. But the important service is the whorehouse.

There are different types of prostitutes and different kinds of whorehouses. The whorehouse itself is usually a dummy corporation, set up, say, as an architectural firm. Services are entered as design of lobby, or checking plans, and payment can be made by credit card. A firm can also have an open account.

The women either have college degrees or can talk as if they do. Many of them can speak two or more languages. They are clean, well-bred, and dress in expensive gowns and lingerie. They often serve on a flat fee basis, for example, one to two thousand dollars for the night.

Trysts are held at one of three places. At the whorehouse itself, which is not often done due to the fear of a raid. At the law firm's condominium, owned for the use of clients or partners. Or at the partner's in-town condominium. Partners will usually have the prostitute picked up in a limousine hired by the firm.

A story once made the rounds which went like this. A large firm on open account with one of the more famous whorehouses neglected to pay the end-of-month bill. The next bill arrived (printed out by computer) with a first warning on the bottom. Then another bill, and another. These were unitemized bills for architectural services rendered.

At the end of the fourth unpaid month, the madam herself appeared in the reception area of the firm. She demanded to see the managing partner. Ushered immediately into his office, she tossed her boa across her shoulder and threatened to sue the firm.

One can imagine what a lawyer in that situation would think. The first instinct would be to consider having the madam arrested for trespass and assault, to teach her a lesson for so insulting a large, prestigious, powerful firm. The second thought would be that payment could be avoided and a lawsuit defended on a variety of grounds, including illegality.

And the third thought would be that in all likelihood, the madam, if not represented for free by the members of another large, prestigious, powerful firm, would be immediately picked up by an organization such as the ACLU, where the underpaid staff would have a heyday.

In this instance, at least, the case was promptly settled.

What You Aren't Supposed To Know ...

Footnote:

1. And, if a firm collapses, they will think nothing of promising support staff full salaries and benefits if they only stay on until the dissolution is completed. Then the genetic lawyers will disclaim any responsibility for making the payments, declaring that other matters (such as their division of the spoils) are more "relevant." (Lawyers prefer terming something relevant instead of important, because anything irrelevant is inadmissible in the court of life.)

CHAPTER SEVEN

HEADHUNTERS AND LATERAL
TRANSFERS

Headhunters

At the end of the first year of law practice (assuming you have lasted that long), you will be inundated by phone calls from headhunters. Headhunters are people who sit around in offices that are decorated to imitate law firms. They pore over a variety of listings: who has recently been admitted to the bar; who is listed in Martindale Hubbell; which law firms are in a hiring posture. And then they have their own listings of requests submitted by law firms.

Phone calls will be followed by letters and business cards. Getting rid of headhunters is like getting rid of an insurance salesman. The reason is quite simple: law firms pay headhunters in the area of fifteen percent of a lateral transfer's new salary. The headhunter typically splits the fee fifty-fifty with the headhunter's firm. Assume an associate's salary of eighty thousand dollars, and a headhunter comes up with six thousand dollars for a few minutes worth of work. The average annual income of an active headhunter in a big city is one hundred twenty thousand dollars (which is more than the income of most associates).

The genetic lawyer will never use a headhunter, so this chapter is for the associate who is bound not to succeed. Headhunters are a good way not to succeed. Some are top notch, but you never know you have a top notch headhunter until after the fact -- the same fact that probably led you to a bad headhunter.

. A bad headhunter is someone who thinks only about his or her potential income and not the impact of a mismatch. In other words, a bad headhunter maintains the philosophy of a genetic lawyer. The

PROFILES OF WHAT ....

A HEADHUNTER IS

A lawyer who worked for a few years at a firm and couldn't hack it.

Someone capable of going down a list of names, placing calls, promising the world, not delivering as promised, accepting the large fee anyway, and sleeping at night.

A person or agency who or which places ads in various law journals describing the years of service (always cumulative if there is more than one headhunter, as in Over One Hundred Years of Graceful Service to the Legal Community), the confidentiality of the process, the careful screening, and how the headhunters are all lawyers (never former lawyers, but lawyers).

THE LAWYER A HEADHUNTER WILL HANDLE

Any litigator (since there is always a demand for this dime-a-dozen crowd to fill in during large cases).

Any third to sixth year associate in non-litigation departments, because having worked at one firm for three or more years shows stability, while a sixth year associate is still not quite near enough to a partnership determination to make him suspect. Besides, senior associates bring in a larger fee.

Any partner having a client base worth over two hundred fifty thousand dollars a year.

Overall, someone with at least some of the following credentials: a ranked law school degree; law review; ivy league undergraduate; clerkship with a federal judge; a current annual income of $80,000 or more.

THE LAWYER THE HEADHUNTER WILL LAUGH OUT THE DOOR

An associate with more than seven years of service at the same firm -- this person is suspect since at partnership level. Exception: a litigator who can be hired to handle a case and then fired.

An associate who has moved from firm to firm more than twice, since this shows instability, even though the moves were at the prompting of the headhunter.

Overall, someone with any of the following credentials: an unranked law school; practicing at Legal Aid or for a sole practitioner; current annual income equivalent to a train conductor; not owning Bally shoes (in black); an earring in the left ear (for a man).

reason for this is simple -- most bad headhunters are either lawyers who didn't make it but, instead of leaving the law, take pleasure in manipulating lawyers who might yet make it; or, they are married to lawyers who didn't make it and they see their low-salaried spouse in every applicant.

The following examples are meant as road signs to the bad headhunter.

The headhunter who keeps placing associates with a partner who goes through a new associate every year. The headhunter will not forewarn you since her fee is irrevocably vested if an associate survives six months (if the headhunter guarantees the placement at all).

The headhunter who does a mass mailing of the associate's resume, thereby making the associate look desperate (word does get around) and cutting off the use of another headhunter (who will not want to send a resume where it has already been).

The headhunter who sends a resume without also calling up the hiring partner and pressing the associate's case. You might as well send the resume yourself, since it has the same likelihood of being looked at.

The headhunter who knows you are working with other head-hunters. Since headhunters often carry the same list of openings, it is inevitable that you will have to tell a headhunter at some time that another headhunter has already sent your resume to Firm X. The headhunter will promptly send your resume to Firm X and insist on fee splitting with the other headhunter, or no interview.

The headhunter who does get you interviews at firms, but neglects to tell you or the firm that there can never be a match. For example, if a firm is looking for someone with experience in creditors' rights or trial practice, and you are a tax lawyer, it is doubtful that an offer is going to be made. Why does that situation occur in the first place? Probably because you are one of the few associates stupid enough to use that headhunter and he or she has to send some sort of body over to the firm.

A bad headhunter will neglect your wishes in other ways, too. For example, if you want to transfer to a corporation, the bad

---

**WHY AN ASSOCIATE WILL NEVER TELL YOU
WHY YOU SHOULD NOT ACCEPT A JOB OFFER
AT HIS FIRM**

You might be a spy sent by his firm's partner who wants additional information for giving the associate a bad evaluation.

You might be interviewing for the spot which will force you to work for the partner everyone hates and the sooner you come on board, the easier life will be for everyone else.

The associate knows that you will not be put in his office or given his secretary to share; or, he knows that you will be going to another department, and therefore will not be competing with him.

The associate is himself on the verge of leaving and thinks it hilarious that you want to come into a firm which has a high turnover rate.

---

headhunter will send you to firms anyway, telling you that the corporations have no current openings. The truth is that having you transfer to a corporation means a lower fee, since corporate salaries are lower than law firm salaries.

Lateral Transfers

Lateral transfers, regardless of their law school class, will find that their past record is still considered relevant. Interviews always open with the following questions: What were your grades at law school; what was your rank; were you on law review? Some interviewers go so far as to request a copy of your transcript and

133

WHY LATERAL TRANSFERS DON'T WORK OUT

You will be ignored by the other associates of your class in the firm because you are competition.

You will be ignored by all other associates in the firm because those who started practice in the firm will have their own schedules, habits and friends; and those who transferred in before you will believe that since it took them two to three years to become socially accepted, it should take you that long.

The old-guard partners you are assigned to work for will constantly nitpick at your work because you are not home grown. Their comments will invariably be, "If you had been trained by this firm from the start, you would be worth your salt by now." (Partners would prefer paying associate salaries in salt.)

In many instances, there will not be office space for you and you will find yourself set up in the library, or in the new wing where construction is still going on. The farther away you are from your department, the more difficult it will be to integrate.

LSAT score.

Otherwise, the interviews follow a pattern similar to that already experienced during the second and third years of law school. There will be an initial interview, during which the attorney will present the firm as being the best firm in the world; a repartee by the associate explaining that he is the best associate in the world; an insightful question by the interviewer as to why the attorney wants to transfer;

and an insightful response that one would be an idiot not to want to transfer to this wonderful new firm.

In short, the interview will be based on lies, inferences, and exaggerations if the associate is anxious about getting a call back (where he will be grilled by six partners and four associates with the exact same sets of questions and wanting to hear the exact same set of answers).

The truth is that an associate does not transfer laterally unless: 1) his present firm stinks; 2) he hates the partners he is working for; 3) he has been told to leave.

If an associate tells an interviewer any of those reasons, he will not be called back. For one, the partner will immediately conclude that any associate willing to relate tales of how awful a firm or partner is will do the same concerning any firm.[1]

For another, if the associate explains that he was, say, fired because the partner is irrational and has a history of firing associates, the interviewer will hear only that the associate was fired. No one wants to hire dead wood.

The lateral transferee, of course, wants to elicit as much information as he can about the type of work he will be doing, for whom he will be doing it, and what kind of personalities he will be going up against. But he cannot ask those questions outright, even though the story on the other side probably involves the lateral transfer of the associate our interviewee may be replacing because that associate could not stand the partners, the firm, or was fired by an irrational partner.

The real test comes at lunch time. A partner and an associate take you downstairs to a relatively expensive restaurant. Menus are handed out. The waiter clears his throat and says to the partner, "Would you like a drink?"

The partner and his associate promptly turn their gazes to the interviewee and say simultaneously, "Would you like a drink?"

It is up to you. The possibility of success or failure hinges on how you handle the otherwise simple question of, Do you want that Absolut on the rocks that you have been craving since nine this morning, or do you order Seltzer with a twist?

135

BLACKLISTING

Lawyers seem attracted to causes involving blacklisting, whether it is of people (Roy Cohn and the McCarthy era) or magazines (The Meese Commission and *Playboy*). They also like blacklisting lateral transfers who don't work out.

Here is the scenario: The partner or partners of the department decide they need some new bodies around and they contact headhunters. The headhunters send over dozens of bodies. The partners are forced to give up pressing work to take these potential associates to expensive lunches or dinners. If that's not bad enough, the partners then have to meet over an expensive lunch or dinner to discuss how the interviews went and who should get a call back.

That's hundreds of firm dollars and lots of hours down the drain. Then there are the call backs, and the partners have to go out to lunch or dinner again.

Finally, the decision is made and the transfer(s) hired. A huge fee is paid to the headhunter, who immediately books a flight to Madrid. It is assumed that the transfer will automatically integrate into the firm, both socially and legally. But what if the associate is lodged in the new wing, half a block away from everyone else? And what if the writing style he or she learned at the old firm is not the one used at the new firm? And what if the associate was hired on the premise that he or she would be doing a certain type of work, but instead the firm decides that the new body will be doing work with which the associate is unfamiliar?

After awhile, the partners decide that the associate is

not going to work out. The associate is given notice. The associate returns to the sun-tanned headhunter and says, What now? The headhunter points out that since the associate was only at the new firm for a few months, it will be impossible to place the associate elsewhere because half a year at one place, and two at another, show instability. Besides, the partners at the new firm have announced that they will not give the associate a good recommendation.

Quite simply, the associate is blacklisted. Whereas a year before, this same associate had to hang up on zealous headhunters and had hundreds of lucrative offers to choose from, he now finds that headhunters won't handle him and that work in a firm or corporation is unavailable.

If in doubt, order a white wine spritzer. Otherwise, go with the odds, and the odds favor sitting straight up in your chair, clasping your hands before you, and saying in a deep, loud voice, "Yes, I'll have Glenlivet straight up." Using an expensive brand name is part of the game.

In other instances, a senior associate or partner will immediately answer the first part of the test question for you and observe your actions while under fire. In one example, the senior associate at a large, prestige firm set an interview time of eight o'clock on a weekday night. The place was a popular pub. Neither associate had eaten when they were seated at the senior associate's favorite and habitual table. While the waiter hovered, the senior associate bluntly said, "What will you have ... to *drink*?"

The associate quickly replied, "Vodka ... on the rocks ... no twist."

The senior associate nodded, saying, "I'm beginning to like you." But he did not order and the waiter did not move away. Both waiter and senior associate seemed to be waiting for something more. Finally, the senior associate grunted and said,

"What brand?"

"Oh. Sorry. Make that ... uh ... Absolut."

The senior associate smiled broadly, clapped his hands together, and said, "The same." To the associate, he added: "Yep, you are my type a guy."

Ten drinks a piece later and still no food, the associate had been informed in explicit detail of the senior associate's and senior partner's sexual exploits, how awful the department's other senior associate was, and had been queried on his own sexual activity. A couple of more drinks were swallowed before the senior associate fumblingly took out the firm's American Express card and charged the one hundred fifty dollar bill. His parting words were,

"We could ush someone like you in the department. Ash far ash I'm consherned, you're hired!"

If you were not asked to leave your present firm, you will, of course, have to lie at your firm with regard to why you are taking long breakfasts or lunches. Common lies are: "I am having root canal on all of my teeth"; "My mother died last week and my father died this week and my wife is in intensive care"; "I have cancer and have to go in for radiation treatments"; and "I don't know what it is, but friends of mine from elementary school keep dropping by."

Eventually, even if you were just testing the waters and actually like your present firm, the fact that your billable hours have fallen off and that you are never around for partners to see you means that you definitely do have to switch to another firm, especially before the next evaluation.

Besides, during this crucial period of a major life-decision, the helpful headhunter is calling every hour on the hour to assess the situation. She doesn't even hide who she is from the message center or your secretary. A bad headhunter will even go a step further -- she will contact the managing partner and suggest that he start looking for an associate of your class and department, "Just in case something should happen in your own department." Hint, hint.

The final test arrives when a firm makes you an offer. Offers are contingent upon recommendations. Recommendations have to come from partners at your present firm. You probably have things you want to hide from the other firm which, although fully defensible, are not things the new firm wants to hear. The new firm wants to hear statements that will lead the partners there to believe that they are stealing away an associate whose absence could very well destroy the losing firm.

You approach the partner who has always said to you that you are brilliant and he, after his initial feigned shock, agrees to give you a wonderful recommendation. Later, a partner from the other firm will call up and say, "Partner X said you were brilliant but also said you had had some troubles with a certain footnote and a memo involving jumping ship. I find those matters troublesome."

In short, you never know what a partner is going to say on the phone about you until it is too late. Odds are that they will say something glowing and something negative, because they want to maintain relations with you in the event you take off and because they want to show the other firm that their firm is not losing a star.

If everything goes well and the offer is confirmed, you may discover that your firm has decided to make a counteroffer. You won't have to work anymore with the partner you hate; you can go to that seminar on ERISA in Hawaii; the partners won't glance at their watches when you go home before eight at night. In every instance I know of where an associate decided to accept the counteroffer and stay with his firm, the associate was forced out of his firm within a year. Remember, you tried leaving them (you selected another firm as being better than theirs!) and no one's going to forget it -- with the exception that you can always return to a firm you left if you do so as a partner with a lucrative client base.

How Much Greener That Grass Really Is

Everyone is beside themselves with joy at the move, right? The partner(s) and associates at your new firm take you out to a celebratory lunch and toast you repeatedly. Your new secretary brings you

139

more office supplies than you've seen in your life. Your income is up ten thousand. You are issued credit cards and a speakerphone. Associates and partners in other departments crowd around to listen to your war stories. The promises made by the partner(s) concerning the types of matters you would be handling are fulfilled from day one. The managing partner of your old firm keeps calling to beg you to come back. The associates in your previous department sob on the phone at your good fortune. The headhunter sends you a fruit basket and an engraved watch.

In your dreams, perhaps, but not in reality. Your old firm will completely ignore you. Everyone at the new firm will ignore you except when you have to work together on a matter. The headhunter will call only to remind you that you have to stay at the new firm for six months for her to collect her entire fee (otherwise, she suggests she might hold you responsible). You won't be assigned a secretary, your office will be in some makeshift corner (if not the library), you won't have any furniture, and that increase in salary is pure tax dollars, never to be heard from again.

What about the promises that probably had more to do with your move than anything else? That you could change departments, or handle matters more to your liking, or go to court? They won't be kept. Your options are to complain and be blacklisted within the firm prior to being fired; to keep quiet, wait a year, and transfer yet again; to quit (which means forgetting about working at a law firm); or to threaten a lawsuit.

Pity that lawyers cannot contract for job descriptions and security. But law firms, like law schools, hire under the employment-at-will doctrine. Everyone is an independent contractor.

What the lateral transferee soon realizes is that, unlike the headhunter's statements that the grass is greener on the other side (for headhunters, anyway), and unlike the partner's promises about work and security, the new firm is just like the old firm, and every firm is the same as every other firm. The decor may be different, the client base may be different, there may be a different emphasis on training techniques, but life in a firm is unchanging.

Footnote:

1. The interviewing partner will, however, press the prospective associate for gossip. In some instances, he will wheedle and plead much like a child, swearing up and down that it won't affect the interview itself (although it will), and that the partner will keep the gossip secret, cross his heart and hope to die (he won't). Genetic lawyers love the sense of gloating more than sex, and gossip is the stuff of gloating.

CHAPTER EIGHT

PARTNERSHIP TRACK

Boredom Settles In

If you survive the first two years of being an associate, you will enter the third year slump that continues until you are a senior associate. In general, this slump arises from the realization that the practice of law is boring and repetitive to the extent that a monkey trained in Pavlovian responses could do it better than you.

This boredom is partly the result of how associates are used in departments. By the third year, you have become acquainted with most of the forms, documents, and cases used in the law and are capable of handling cases on your own. But if you were allowed to handle cases on your own, that would imply that you were ready for partnership. Since that just cannot be in the cards for a few more years, you have to continue wading through the same old stuff under the same supervision.

In most litigation departments, for example, a junior associate will have no or very little courtroom experience until he is a senior associate. At that stage, he will be granted a five minute oral argument in a five hundred dollar case.

No Vacation

The slump is also a result of not having had a vacation for three years. Law firms are always very good about stating (orally) that you have four weeks of vacation a year, and are always very good at insisting that you are too indispensable to take a vacation, even if your demise is being plotted. Strangely enough, while you are missing your vacation time and billing more hours, you are not

143

packing away all those weeks for a later year -- vacation time has to be taken during its allotted year, or it is lost forever.

Partners, on the other hand, never miss a vacation. In fact, it often seems that they get to use associate vacation time accruing to their department.

Turnover

If you are a lawyer-not-to-be, you will be affected by the revolving doors that surround you and through which pass your friends. Those name plates outside of each office are purposely designed so that they can be snapped off the wall. Another emotionally exhausting aspect of losing friends is realizing that you will never see them again because, once someone leaves a firm, it is as if he had never existed. You only have the time to socialize with the lawyers around you and, after a few years, there will be no one around anymore whom you recognize.

Politicking For Partnership

The genetic lawyer will be enjoying himself immensely. Not only will he be feverishly politicking the right partners, he will also have himself elected to the various committees partners permit the associates to organize. This means that he can call associate luncheons once every other month and dominate the conversation and then report back to the partners as to which associates he likes and dislikes.

A regular junior associate will additionally begin to sense the absurdity of being a lawyer in the economic sense. As much as he feels that he is being overpaid, he will find himself caught up in the annual *cause celebre* of what other firms are giving their associates. Associates, on their own time, will call associates at other firms and draw up complicated charts showing salary increases, bonuses, and fringe benefits. A lawyer-not-to-be will be elected to present this chart to the partners' Committee on Compensation, which will then send a partner to an associates' luncheon to state, orally, that the Committee is closely studying the issue. That means the matter is closed until the following year and that the associate who presented the chart will not make partner.

Another absurdity that will confront junior associates is the annual evaluation of partners by associates. This occurs in those firms which consider themselves "liberal" or "avant garde" and which provide associate retreats, in-house shrinks, and free soda. Junior associates recognize that these evaluations are not only meaningless, but dangerous, for it is a simple enough matter for a partner to find out the source of any comment felt to be derogatory. Besides, the senior associate who is up for partner in a department, and who has the final edit of the partner's evaluation, will rewrite any negative statements so that, when the evaluation is read at yet another associates' luncheon, it will appear that his department contains the most beloved partner.

Alternatively, a senior associate will use partner evaluations to his own purposes, by permitting a competing senior or junior associate to include statements as to how the partner could change for the better. At the meeting where these statements are read aloud, it will be that other associate who has the honor. *Ipso facto*, the competition suddenly disappears.

At the last moment, a junior associate will realize that he is part of an experiment wherein his competition is seated in electric chairs and he is at a table containing the switch giving electric shocks. The genetic senior associate and partner are standing behind him and, when they say give a shock, he presses the switch. When the final order comes to give the shock that can cause death, the junior associate will flinch for a moment, and then pull the switch. In his mind, however, he will visualize not only members of his class, but also the senior associate, burning and trembling from the electrical charge. Thus, another senior associate is born who is on partnership track.

145

What You Aren't Supposed To Know ...

Acceptance By Partners

At this stage, you will also discover what being integrated into firm life really means. Firm life means gossip. At lunch, for example, you will be entertained by the following kind of witty conversation:

PARTNER: I lost my virginity when I was fifteen [or thirteen, or seven]. The woman's name was Marge and she was seventeen [or twenty or thirty]. She was six feet tall, had long blond hair, blue eyes, beautiful lips, big tits, ha, ha, ha. I taught her a lot. She said so. She's a movie actress and model now. Very famous.

It should be noted that the partner saying this is inevitably short, megalocephalic, has carbuncles on his fingertips, and bad breath. Older partners can be even worse -- lawyers age in a manner that would frighten even Dorian Gray. Hair sprouts like wires from ears, nostrils, and palms; liver spots swim across crinkly skin; eyes gloss over with a blue haze; and warts march across lips and fingers.
Let's move on to a luncheon with two partners.

PARTNER 1: And then there was Brigitte. She was that tall blond at X firm, before I left. A model. I took photographs of her. She autographed them.

PARTNER 2: And you still have them in the drawer, right?

PARTNER 1: Right.

PARTNER 2: I'm surprised your girlfriend hasn't found them. By the way, did you notice that new girl, what's her name?

PARTNER 1: Pat? Oh, I'm already into her pants. The first day she arrived. In fact, she came onto me.

PARTNER 2: But she's been coming onto me, too. I don't believe it. Look, we have to compare notes.

146

The proudest moments are the extramarital affairs.

PARTNER: And then, after the party, I drove Stephanie home. I thought it was the only decent thing to do.

NAIVE ASSOCIATE: You weren't married then?

PARTNER: Of course I was. And I had to drive Partner Y home, too. So we were all in the car and Stephanie asked us up to her apartment ...

NAIVE ASSOCIATE: The two of you?

PARTNER: Of course. I was up for partnership then.

NAIVE ASSOCIATE: Partner Y is the head of your department, isn't he?

PARTNER: You know, you ask really dumb questions. Anyway, there we are in Stephanie's apartment and we were all pretty drunk anyway, so ...

In-house hanky panky is, nonetheless, a good industry. Partners rarely discuss their families. In fact, if a partner is going to discuss any aspect of his family, it is going to be a current divorce. Partners like to think of their firms as their families. The only time a wife is important is when the wife is the daughter of a partner or judge, and then she retains her importance only until the lawyer becomes a partner. Notice that only partners have locks on their doors. They have the most attractive secretaries. Notice that those secretaries wear expensive jewelry. If you have moral qualms, suppress them. What the Pope doesn't know won't hurt him. You love it all; it's a big kick; you want to do the same.

Those on partnership track also realize that being seen is more

HOW TO BECOME A PARTNER

Marry the daughter of Someone. Someone being: a federal judge; a famous practitioner; anyone wealthy; the head of a medium to large-sized corporation; the founder of the firm.

Make the rounds of partners two to three times a day telling bawdy jokes, kibbitzing, and asking about the family.

Start wearing the same color, cut, and brand name clothes and shoes as the senior partner in your department.

Spread rumors about associates in your class.

Take credit for every case that ends well; blame competing associates for every screw-up.

If things aren't going well, take off a year to work at the U.S. Attorneys Office, then return to the firm with yet another diploma for the wall.

Never tell competing associates the actual facts or issues of a case if they are assigned to help you out.

Tell competing associates that the senior partner has said that they can leave early, then you remain and walk out with the partner, complaining about how all the others have left early.

Share a woman with a senior partner.

Procure women for the senior partner.

Write articles and books for publication under the name of the senior partner and insist that receiving a minor credit doesn't really matter to you. Of course, the actual writing and researching will be done by other associates and paralegals under your supervision.

Ensure that you attend every outing, luncheon, dinner, or party at which important partners will make an appearance. Dance with their wives. Pat the heads of children.

Avoid female partners. For the most part, these first generation lawyers will be extremely irascible, feeling they have to prove themselves to be men at every moment.

Get out of the litigation department.

Act as a chauffeur, losing tennis or racquet ball opponent, and drinking buddy for senior partners.

Befriend the senior partner's secretary, buy her roses and chocolates, and hope that she puts in a good word for you.

Stake out the senior partner's office so that whenever you see a competing associate entering the office you can fly in breathlessly, holding hundreds of pages of irrelevant documents, and announce that you have just settled a case, rammed some point down an opponent's throat, or saved the department from embarrassment (caused by the intruding associate).

Be the offspring of Someone.

If a female, go to bed with the senior partner, but this can sometimes backfire. Example: the senior partner suddenly ends up on the outs with the firm because he has not brought in enough clients, or has lost a major client because of something he said or ate. He will then announce that it was all your fault because you distracted him, and you will be given notice.

Change your name so that it sounds as if you are a prime cut of meat.

Bring in the family business.

For women: glory in the wet T-shirt contests; have a nose job and breast implant; stop wearing bras; don't cross your legs unless you are wearing a slit skirt.

Perform a coup, such as bringing in a Japanese client (the most lucrative and hardest to catch).

Become the same height and weight as the senior partner; dye your hair the same color; marry his ex-wife to stop alimony payments.

important than doing good legal work. Being seen means coming in on weekends when there is no work to do, just to make sure that any partners who have come in see you. Then you go home, leaving the light on in your office. Leaving lights on in offices is important, especially if you are gone.

Politicking additionally means having no fear of bathrooms. A great many important conversations occur in bathrooms. An associate joining a partner for a piss, urinal to urinal. An associate joining a partner, stall to stall. An associate just standing outside of the stall, speaking to the partner within. "How are you, Joe? Wanted to speak to you about case X. How's the divorce? Good, good."

Indeed, no personal function is sacrosanct in a large law firm. This is because of two things: loudspeakers and messengers. If, at any time during the day, you decide to snooze or scratch your crotch, it is inevitable that a messenger will walk in at that moment. And if you go to the bathroom and are not in deep discussion with another attorney, it is inevitable that the loudspeaker in the bathroom will call out your name and insist on your dialing in promptly.

The genetic lawyer understands the value of everything that will get his name circulated. He will have relatives call the firm to have him paged, and he will circulate memos consisting of newspaper clippings and jokes just to ensure that his name is on some piece of mail reaching every partner twice a day.

Being on partnership track is also very similar to following the allegorical changes detailed in *Animal Farm*. Tall associates, over the years, will become short if the powerful attorney is short. Short associates will become tall. Fat associates will become thin, thin ones fat. Happily married associates will divorce and, if possible, move in with the partner and make love to the same women. These partners-to-be will model their personalities after the partner's. The adage that if Partner X is nasty, therefore all of Partner X's predecessors and successors were or will be nasty, is true.

Looking and acting like the powerful partner has its advantages in that the partner begins to believe that he has a protégé who can do no wrong. That belief is essential to the partner-to-be because he will begin making mistakes. He will make mistakes because he forgets to bluff on occasion; or because he is spending too much time telling dirty jokes to other partners; or because he is worrying too much about competition. The senior partner, however, will graciously forgive the senior associate his errors (as long as the client picks up the tab) and blame it on whomever the senior associate fingers. That will usually be everyone else in the world.

Using Scapegoats As Ladder Rungs

Senior associates, besides pandering and joke-telling, will file their nails on junior associates. If something goes wrong, it has to be someone's fault, and junior associates are good scapegoats because: 1) they have little contact with the partner and won't know about being a scapegoat until the annual evaluation (if not fired before then); 2) a whiz kid junior associate represents competition to a senior associate because the partner can elect to pass over the latter to wait for the former. When in doubt, get rid of the competition.

In this situation, call the junior associate Z, and the senior associate, X.

Z points out to X that X has neglected to serve papers within the time limit. X turns bright red, tells Z he'll take care of it, and then runs into Partner's office and complains that Z has forgotten about the time limit and X will have to work overtime to get Z out of this mess. On top of that, Z will be taken off the case at X's insistence.

Next week, Z will point out to X that X has neglected the rule against perpetuities with regard to a certain matter. X will rush off to Partner and complain that Z is ranting and raving over an imaginary area of the law and is probably mentally unsound. Z will be taken off that case.

Later, Partner will point out to X that the client has called and asked how the settlement is going. X will realize that he has forgotten completely about the settlement and that the cut-off date for negotiations has passed. Client has lost three million dollars unless something can be salvaged. But X's first response will be that Z was handling the matter and X will have to bail him out yet again. Z will be removed from the matter even though he was never involved with it in the first place.

Eventually, Z will have only a matter or two and will be called into Partner's office. Partner will say, "We have been extremely upset with your work and, indeed, I have spoken with all the other partners in the firm and the consensus is that you are incompetent. Moreover, you are not holding up your end in terms of work load. You have two months to find another job -- but not as a lawyer."

X, by this time, has rationalized to himself that the source of all his problems really is Z. Partner has also been convinced that Z is a trouble maker and really is incompetent. Z will discover that not only can he not get interviews at good firms, but that the only firms which will even consider seeing him are located in the Far East and pay one

---

WHAT PARTNERS SAY TO KEEP SENIOR ASSOCIATES WORKING UNTIL PASSED OVER

I haven't given it thought yet.

Really, it's too soon to worry.

Not now. We'll discuss it later.

And how's your family?

Where is it you said you keep your case files and notes?

I must have wax in my ear. Problem at my age. What?

I have heard favorable reports on you.

I haven't seen the latest print-out yet.

We'll be in touch.

Your new secretary's cute. What's her name?

Didn't I just talk to the bank to get you that mortgage approval?

It's up to the committee, you know that.

Have you about finished up your current matters?

HOW LONG IT TAKES TO MAKE PARTNER

It used to be six to seven years. Now it is any length of time established at retreats by subcommittees.

One of the great tricks of the establishment is to change how many years it takes to make partner so that instead of announcing who has made partner, the firm can announce that the new policy, beneficial to all, is that it will now take one, two, three, or four years longer to be up for partnership. The associate is trapped at the firm because he is too senior to move elsewhere without raising eyebrows full of suspicion. And he continues to work at a lower salary than he would otherwise have garnered if he had become a partner.

But whom can you complain to without assuring that you will NOT make partner?

---

tenth his current salary in an unknown currency. Z will begin to think that X and/or Partner are spreading rumors about him. But whom is he going to go to for support? Remember: all partners will stick together, even if one of the partners is an admitted murderer. The only time partners will attack each other is when money is at stake. No confidence is safe with any lawyer since a lawyer will always breach the confidence if he feels that he can use it to political advantage.

Size Advantage And Isolation Factors

Another example involves a department with one partner, two senior associates, and one junior associate. The partner is, say, five feet tall. Senior Associate X is, say, five feet tall (after an operation). Senior Associate Y is six feet tall. Junior associate Z is six feet tall. Y, it turns out, has worked with Partner for six years and written books and articles with him. X has recently come on board, had his shortening operation, and begun to impress himself on Partner. Z, too, has recently come on board but, as a partner not-to-be, begins socializing with Y, who is intelligent, erudite, and an expert in the law -- also a partner not-to-be.

How does X win over Partner? The task is not as hard as it seems. After all, although Y has devoted his legal career to Partner, that is an insufficient reason to believe that Partner feels any allegiance to Y. What X immediately has going for him is his height. Partners tend to like people their same height if their height is at an extreme. Thus, in courtrooms and at depositions and conferences, one often sees lawyers from a firm trooping in and each side will be the same height. One firm, for example, always has partners and associates who average six feet three in height. One other distinguishing characteristic includes beards, but since they can be grown or bought, they are not that important.

Associate X therefore arranges always to stand next to Partner so that Partner can visibly sense how comfortable it is to stand next to someone his own height. After a week of that, X will begin the process of cutting Partner off from everyone else in the department. That means memorizing Partner's arrival and departure times from the office, when he eats, when he goes to the bathroom, when he strolls up and down the hallway. On the selected day, X will appear in Partner's room, bearing a cup of coffee, at exactly the time Partner arrives.

From then on, X will never leave Partner alone or unprotected. If Z or Y want to see Partner, they will find X in Partner's office and X will shoo them away. If Z or Y keep watch and notice X leaving Partner's office, and they approach Partner's closed door, they will find that X is suddenly rushing down the hallway, arms flailing, shooing them away.

Eventually, all work assignments will be given by X and will be funneled back to Partner through X, who will state that the finished work is his alone and what trouble he's having carrying the entire work load for the department but, sigh, someone has to do it. Partner will appreciate the attention and the lightening of his own work load.

X, though, knows that Partner can still pass him over. "Passing over" is the Biblical event where only associates with a streak of blood from other associates on their door are made partner. X, therefore, will devote a great deal of the time he spends with Partner slyly putting down Y and Z -- Z because of the fear that Partner might suddenly decide that Z does good work and can carry the department at an associate level, thereby saving Partner the trouble of making X or Y partner and having someone competing with *him*.

Y, being a senior associate, will sense the change but, worrying more about doing a good job and perhaps believing that six to eight years of devotion has secured him a shot at partnership, will continue to do his work until he notices that not only is Partner cut off from him, but X is telling dirty jokes to the other partners, along with dropping hints that Y does terrible work.

Y will nonchalantly sneak into Partner's room on the one day X is hospitalized for ulcers, and ask Partner about his partnership chances. Partner's response will inevitably be: "I have not given it much thought. That's all I can say about it right now." Y, knowing that all Partner has been thinking about is whether to make someone partner, will immediately begin looking for work elsewhere.

WHEN PARTNERSHIPS ARE ANNOUNCED

During a holiday, such as Thanksgiving or Christmas. This ensures that all senior associates will be present during a paid vacation to accept additional assignments even if they don't make partner.

After senior associates have bought a house or condo, impregnated their wives or mistresses, or otherwise increased indebtedness.

As soon as senior associates have developed heart disease, ulcers, or nervous disorders.

155

The above scenario is actually a redacted version of what often occurs. In many instances, it may be that our Y has been lead counsel on a number of important cases and Partner knows that only Y can successfully bring those cases to completion. The fact that Y has been so successful, however, is also Y's death knell. Partner will say to Y: "You know I cannot commit myself to partnerships right now since it is a group decision among all the partners, but I think it is safe to say that you have nothing to worry about." Y, being devoted to his work, will take Partner's words as words of assurance and, besides putting in even longer hours, will purchase a home and get his wife pregnant: the two earmarks of a senior associate who believes he is on partnership track.

Retreats

Associates are selected for partnership at "retreats." The partners rent a hotel, motel, or country club for a weekend and read reports about profits, salaries, and client bases, and then put associates on the table for partnership consideration. Regardless of a partner's statement that the selection process is a group decision, it isn't. It is up to partners to propose associates from their own departments, and the proposal itself is worth a great deal of weight. The only matter of concern to the other partners is whether making the associate a partner will drain or increase the partnership kitty.

The Monday after such retreats is a busy day for ambulance services. Our Y is of course passed over and everyone will know because the names of the new partners are sent around to everyone. If a senior associate's name is not on the memo, he is not a partner. And that is the way they find out themselves, since the partners only call in advance those senior associates who have made partner.

Y will collapse at his desk and be carted off on a stretcher. Y's wife will have a miscarriage. The bank (a firm client) will bring foreclosure proceedings against Y's new house. From them on, Y will walk with a slight limp and a hunch in his shoulders. His skin will always be pasty and moist. He will have interminable intestinal problems.

Since Z had befriended Y and is the same height as Y, Z will begin seeking employment elsewhere.

X, on the other hand, will begin coming to work late and leaving early and will ignore Partner and begin spreading rumors among the other partners that he has been carrying Partner all these years and what the department needs is good, young blood. What X means by that is that he should be made sole partner in the department and permitted to hire a new junior associate who will be female, from an unranked law school, and untrained in the area of law practiced in the department.[1]

For the lawyer who definitely is not going to succeed, being passed over can occur early in a career. Z is one example. Another example is just the fact of working at a large sweatshop. Sweatshops are those firms where associates never see the sun, never feel the wind on their cheeks, and survive on coffee and potato chips. There are cots in each room and shower stalls in the bathrooms. Most of these associates will burn out after a year or two and will end up driving cabs and *Good Humor* trucks. They will never be able to complete a sentence without stuttering and falling silent. They won't care about sex. Their hands will shake. They will have pimples. They will have permanent bags under their eyes. And, like lemmings, they will jump ship at the same time each year (after being told that they will be pushed if they don't jump).

The Passed Over

For those of you who live in cities with subway systems, you may have noticed of late that a new scam has been developed. This consists of bums entering a subway car and saying: My name is Jim. I was just released from X Prison. I do not want to rape or murder or steal or create general mayhem, but I am hungry and I cannot get a job. I want to stay clean. I do not want to hurt anyone. Your contributions will help me keep straight.

Last week, I saw an associate who had been passed over for

partnership entering my subway car. He was dressed like a bum. I was about to greet him when he announced: My name is Bill. I was just passed over for partner at a major law firm. I do not want to be forced into starting my own firm, commingling funds, or inflicting boiler-plate clauses on your daughters, but I am hungry and cannot get a regular job. I want to stay clean. I don't want to defraud anyone. Your contributions will help me stay away from the law.

Bill was given a tremendous amount of cash by the frightened passengers.

The nagging question in the law is, Where do all those associates passed over for partnership go? I always believed there was an island somewhere to which they were sent. An island that would have made Kafka proud, where the lawyers are strapped to a large, wood machine that runs needles over their shivering, naked bodies, stamping them with the words: I Could Not Make Partner. How can they face their families or friends again? How can they begin a new life in middle age?

Partners Can Get Sacked

If there is any consolation to not making partner, it is that law firms have started to fire partners.

It had always been accepted that there would be power struggles among partners. Sometimes, these struggles occur posthumously, as where a firm votes to delete a partner's name from the firm's name. In many cases, the partner will have been dead so long that no one can remember what he did around the place, but deleting his name will mean opening a slot to be used in enticing a big, live name to the firm, while perhaps ending any monetary obligations the firm might have had to the partner's widow.

A more common struggle takes place when the senior partner refuses to move out. This senior partner is usually senile and serves no function other than to eat all the cashews at the weekly cocktail party. Two or more camps will be formed within the firm, each headed by a partner wanting to become senior partner through a *coup d'état.* The plans are the same. As soon as the senior partner goes to the hospital or on a vacation, the camps alert their members and there is a mad dash to the senior partner's office, which is always the largest corner office in the firm. At the head of each camp is the potential replacement; behind him, his followers carrying his furniture.

As the camps bear down on each other with the force of a ton of wood, flesh, and bone, one camp might falter and fall to the wayside. Another might suddenly vote to negotiate. Or, there might actually be a dizzying crash. In any event, only one camp will win and when the senior partner returns with a tan or a row of stitches where his prostate used to be, he will go to his office and discover that he has been deposed. A security guard will escort him to the back exit.

The big change, however, is in the trend toward firing partners. Not for incompetence, mind you. In fact, partners incompetent to practice law are often highly regarded since they are the ones who have a knack for finding and bringing in clients. These types of partners tend to be ex-politicians.

The partners who get sacked are the ones who do not generate enough income to satisfy the other partners. The departments most heavily hit are Litigation, and Trusts and Estates.

If there were any real justice, these sackings would occur across the board on Christmas Day right after the partners to be fired have extended their credit to the limit by purchasing condos for their mistresses.

What You Aren't Supposed To Know ...

Footnotes:

1. New partners get offices with locks on the doors; the right to hire their secretaries; the right to select new associates to work with. Income doesn't increase that much unless a partner has his own client base and negotiates a share differing from that of other new partners. To give you some idea about the odds of becoming a partner at a prestige firm, the myriad of statistics present this picture: approximately nine percent of associates make partner. Of that nine percent, less than two percent represent women and blacks. In a class of twenty associates, therefore, less than two will be made partner, with one finger being female and the small toe black. Moreover, becoming a partner starts the round of politicking all over again -- partners, like associates, are new, junior, senior, and senile. As discussed in the previous chapter with regard to associates, partners, too, are sought out by headhunters promising greener pastures -- as long as the partner has a client base grossing no less than $250,000 a year.

CHAPTER NINE

COMMITTEES, COMPUTERS, AND CONTENTIONS

Committees

Large law firms form large committees. Committees spawn subcommittees. Subcommittees appoint task forces. Task forces hire experts who are usually related to important partners. Experts hire children, nephews, and nieces. A report is written. The report is read to the task force. The task force spends a month rewriting the report and presents it to the subcommittee. The subcommittee spends two months arguing over the report, and then another two months rewriting it for presentation to the committee. The committee members argue so vehemently over the report that they cannot rewrite it, so each member submits his own report to a joint committee of committees. Since by then no one has any idea as to what the original topic was, all the reports are tabled and the meeting is adjourned for a dinner on the firm.

This is one reason why large law firms can gross millions and millions of dollars a year, and yet have net profits in the two to five percent range.

The bottomline has two prongs: lawyers are genetically incapable of coming to agreement on any matter unless there is something in it for them; and lawyers are terrible businessmen.

Computers

Although there are a string of good examples as to how lawyers screw up the business side of a firm, computerization is perhaps the

161

best example because law firms purport nowadays to be able to give clients advice on technological matters.

At one large firm, the issue of computerization went down through the various subcommittees to the task force. The expert who was hired was an interior designer. The reason for this was that the firm had just spent a million dollars remodeling and the thought was that a computer is a computer, let's get a system that matches the decor.

And they did.

At another firm, the task force decided that the primary concern with computers was having not just one failsafe system, but five. What it did was to purchase a huge system composed of terminals and minicomputers, each of which supposedly contained five back-up chips so that if one failed, the next one would step in, and so on. They paid more than five times the price of what they would have paid for what they thought was the poorly designed IBM or DEC (which weren't clients anyway). Then they paid another couple of hundred thousand to have their data transferred to the new system. Lo and behold, during the first real crush weekend where a dozen SEC filings had to be finished, this wonderful, spectacular, eternal system irrevocably crashed.

Well, then, what about those systems that advertise in the law journals as being made just for law firms? Many firms pick Door Number One, or Two, or Three. And what they often get is a micro-computer made up of parts from other computers without enough memory to compose even one page of a document and with a printer that chatters away like a client opening a bill. The firm discovers that: 1) it must pay twice the going price for diskettes that are "specially" formatted just for that system; 2) it must pay a hundred times the going price for a "special" board that will expand memory enough so that a document can actually be written; 3) it must pay four hundred dollars for a "special" soundproof cabinet for the printer; and 4) the supplier is going out of business anyway.

To vendors of no-name computer systems and developers of untested software, law firms are considered the suckers of the trade. Not only will they be persuaded by the color selection of the computers (and, God knows, you don't get color choice from IBM, DEC, WYSE, Compaq, HP, or other manufacturers of real computers), but lawyers don't know the questions to ask and often hire consultants who receive kickbacks from the no-names.

Even worse, lawyers don't renegotiate the contracts they are going to sign! They swallow a buyer beware and suffer the consequences.

The best story is one observable at many of the large firms. The "word processing" systems these firms buy require the following steps to get a document outputted:

1. The lawyer dictates or writes out a document.

2. The secretary types out the document on an IBM Selectric using a certain print ball.

3. This typed document is then scanned and digitized -- that is, the pages are fed into a machine that reads the text, converting it into a code acceptable to the computer.

4. A (human) word processor then pulls up the document and checks to make sure the text was scanned and digitized without error.

5. The word processor prints out the document which, with the typed version, is returned to the lawyer.

6. The lawyer proofs the document, making changes using a red pen. If there are a lot of changes, his secretary will have to type out the changes using the special print ball.

7. These materials are then returned to word processing. Typed changes are scanned and digitized and the word processor then pulls the changes into the previously saved file.

8. The new document is printed out and returned to the lawyer.

This process can go on forever. One might suggest that lawyers be given their own terminals or microcomputers, so that lawyers could directly input, correct, and print out documents. These desk computers could also be used as terminals for computerized law searches, for sending electronic mail, and for maintaining calendars.

The answer at most firms is no. Lawyers do not type, they dictate. (It should be noted that most partners are from a generation which has a tremendous fear of computers. These partners also have a fear of being shown up by associates. If all lawyers had computers on their desks, they would supposedly have to be used. Partners would not be able to live buying something useless for them but helpful to associates.)

Then what about computers for each secretary? But that would mean storing personal accounts which might be retrieved by roving associates. Typewriters never leave traces.

Besides, the additional time and personnel it takes a firm to get one page printed out is billed to the client. Unlike other industries, where productivity has to be increased to increase profits, law firms make more the slower they go.

Contentions

Other than a partner being sacked, one of the interesting events in the life of a law firm is when a partner, group of partners and associates, or entire departments secede from a firm. The fireworks can be glorious.

A partner leaving is never the issue; the contentions arise over clients, billings, and revenues.[1] The partner and the firm want to retain the money and its source (but not the indebtedness). Neither is going to budge an inch. After all, why should they? Each has free litigation resources at his or its disposal, and having the litigators contribute another ten hours of nonbillable time to a forty-eight hour day means nothing to anyone (not even the litigators, who are already living in a hallucinatory world after the first month on the job).

How, a perceptive client might ask aloud, does it come about that lawyers end up suing each other over matters like clients, billings, and revenues? Aren't law firms professional corporations, modeled after partnerships, and aren't there written articles detailing how these matters of secession should be handled?

Sure, but when has that ever stopped a lawyer from shouting, Sue them!!

So they sue each other. The charges and countercharges are

worth reading. Partner X never fulfilled his obligations to the Firm. Firm Y is guilty of malpractice. I brought in that client! No, I brought that client in! That's my money! X conspired with Partner Z and Associates A, B, and C. Z intentionally interfered with prospective economic advantage by telling potential and actual clients that they would be leaving and the Firm would be unable to handle the matters! He's a liar! No, they're lying!

Of course, these matters are usually settled prior to trial, but not before depositions. A deposition is a pre-trial event where a party or witness is asked questions for a record kept by a stenographer. It is like a mini-trial. There is nothing more fun for a lawyer than to make another lawyer wriggle and sweat. Isn't it true that ...? Didn't you say that ...? (If this actually went to trial, all of the lawyers would be wriggling and sweating.)

The person who will be blacklisted for making a move will be the associate who accompanies the partner. As long as the partner retains some of the clients, billings, and revenues, the new firm will be satisfied -- until the partner decides to move to yet another firm, taking with him the clients, billings, and revenues. But associates who jump ship don't have clients, billings, or revenues; they follow the partner based upon assurances of being taken care of. That is, until the partner opts for another associate who happens to be his height.

Footnotes:

1. Or, in the case of a firm crumbling, responsibility for the debt. The 700-lawyer Finley, Kumble collapsed in late 1987 to the tune of $85 million in debts owed banks. (The banks were not overly happy; they sued the individual partners -- using other large law firms, of course -- and then pushed the firm remains into bankruptcy court.)

CHAPTER TEN

CORPORATE COUNSEL

Corporate counsel have, until recently, lived under a stigma known as corporate counsel. The perception is this: corporate counsel are associates who were passed over for partnership and who chose not to exile themselves on a small, uncharted island off the coast of Florida where all non-genetic lawyers end up. Corporate counsel only work nine to five, five days a week. Corporate counsel never have to do the hard work, which is fielded out to law firms. Corporate counsel have interests outside the law, such as family and literature. Corporate counsel actually make business decisions.

Business Decisions

Let's look at the business decision question first. Lawyers in law firms will do their mad scramble with one or two partners and two or three associates to come up with a "legal analysis" of a potential business decision. This advisory memorandum, as noted previously, will be given to the client written in the subjunctive and the alternative. The sole reason for this process is the fear of malpractice suits. The client, more likely than not, is going to go ahead with his original idea (which, for New Jersey food clients, New York garment center clients, and unions, will generally be: I'm gonna stuff the motha in cement and let him sing to da fishes in da river)(another parenthetical: not to leave out the sophisticated banking client: Well, then, it's settled, we'll take out security interests in the building, fixtures, inventory, goods, and his children and grandchildren and, if he defaults, we'll go in and grab everything we can).

Unfortunately, the concept of giving business advice dressed in would's and could's and or's has developed into a way of life for lawyers. Remember, lawyers run law firms. What most lawyers do not understand is that law firms are a business, like any other. Instead, lawyers run law firms like feifdoms competing with each other, political enclaves known as the Committee on Committees, the Committee on Interior Design, the Committee on Benefits, and so on.

Thus, when a law firm wishes to make a major business decision concerning itself, it hires an outside consultant. These outside consultants are people who realize that law firms can be taken for a lucrative ride. All one has to do is bluff and the lawyers, not able to come to any business decision among themselves, will follow the consultant's advice. That advice usually brings in the consultant's brother-in-law as a vendor, and the brother-in-law's cousin as the repairman, and the cousin's sister-in-law as the Consumer Complaints Division, etc. etc.

Corporate counsel is not like that. The corporation has to decide whether to do X. What is the legal analysis of X, and what are the business ramifications financially, administratively, and competitively? Corporate counsel are executive lawyers and must cope with and comprehend business decisions, often in a brief period. Whereas outside counsel might take a month to answer an issue with a hundred page memorandum, in-house counsel usually have to say something on the spot and then back it up within a day or two.

Some of the questions requiring snap judgments are: Can we copy that ad our competitor just ran? Why can't we give only our best customers this gift or product? Can you make up some cause of action so that we can sue our competitor and not be tossed out of court until they settle in our favor? Will you see to it that I don't have to pay back this personal loan the corporation gave me? Have you finished my taxes yet? Did you set up that trust for my daughter? Where are the copies of those wills you were preparing for the executive vice presidents? Is a mistress deductible?

The big boom in corporate suits has involved interpretations of employment agreements containing restrictive covenants. These clauses say things like: if you leave our employ, you cannot work in the same trade or business in this area (or, anywhere) for the next five years (or, the rest of your natural life); and, anything you learn while in our employ is a proprietary trade secret, and you cannot use that knowledge forever and ever. The breadth and vacuity of these clauses is sufficient for keeping corporate blood at a boiling level, particularly in the high-tech industries.

Politics And Doors

Yet corporations are just as political as law firms. For example, one senior attorney, a renowned alcoholic, used his political muscle to move into a corner office. Unfortunately, he was habituated to the location of his former doorway. Every morning he would proudly stumble toward his new office and crash into the wall. He flexed some more muscle and had his door moved three inches to the right. You can imagine the mess that entailed since it involved a major structural change. Scaffolding went up along the entire hallway. Workers went in and out. Sawdust filled the air. Paint fell on his rug.

Our counsel decided that as long as he had a corner office, a properly placed door, and needed a new rug, he would get an expensive Persian rug. There, he pressed a button too many. The other senior attorneys all got Persian rugs, even though none of them had office furniture that went with floral patterns. The alcoholic attorney responded by getting a color television set and VCR. The others got televisions and VCRs. He got a larger speakerphone. They got speakerphones. And then, one day, he vomited on the wife of the vice president during a party and was never heard from again.

Senior attorney number two used his muscle, called in his cards, and got the corner office. But he was used to his former doorway and kept bumping into the new office's door. The scaffolding went back up.

By the way, an underling sent around a memo suggesting that all offices be formed using partitions that included movable doors.

Just as in a law firm, then, corporate counsel depend upon

political bases and displays of power. In a large city where corporate headquarters occupy an entire skyscraper, the executive offices will be on the top floor, and the attorneys will have the floor directly below.[1]

Budgets And Empires

Corporate counsel also try to argue for larger budgets so that they can expand their departments on the theory that a larger department means a larger power base. And it is true in corporations that a big budget is likely to get bigger, not smaller.

But, unlike a law firm, there has to be a business reason for the expansion, not a legal one. Thus, assume an antitrust case is pending. The rationale given in the budget request will not be that a case is pending, but that litigation support facilities must be expanded which will save money with regard to how much work has to be fielded out to private firms.

Once a budget is approved, the money has to be spent. No one in their right mind in a corporation returns unused funds. Of course, most of the residual funding will go toward moving doors back and forth along hallways, so surpluses are not a great concern.

The great concern is that when the money is spent, it must be in such a manner that no other department can come in and take over the personnel or equipment. On the other hand, those wishing to expand their empires from a smaller base will attempt to unitize procedures. The result is often this: each department will have its own computer system for number crunching and databases that is incompatible with everyone else's computer system, whereas all departments will share a single word processing system. The political power involved in controlling the word processing system is that the system can be programmed to keep track of who is working on what project in which department, how much time secretaries spend inputting and printing out, and when they do it. Power is knowledge and every detail has some use later on.

Win Or Lose

What is the soul behind this competition? Corporate counsel also have a ladder to climb, from attorney, to senior attorney, to general counsel, to secretary and general counsel, to vice president and general counsel, to president and general counsel, all the way up to Chairman of the Board.

An attorney's progression up the ladder depends upon his power base -- and the whims of higher-up executives. For example, one major corporation had an opening at the president level. There were twelve senior general counsel up for the position, all politicking for the position, handing out or promising favors, and pulling in favors. The Chairman, however, had his own power base to worry about and apparently felt that selecting any one of his in-house staff would eventually weaken his own standing. He brought in an outsider.

A large corporation will involve a parent company and a number of divisions and subsidiaries. Those who work as attorneys for the parent company have the plum jobs in that they work for Legal Headquarters, have as a responsibility the supervision of the legal work of attorneys in the subs and divisions, and report directly to the chief executive officers.

Landing the plum job is very similar to pursuing partnership track. You either start out as counsel in Legal Headquarters and then, after a year, are fielded out to a sub or division, or you start out at a sub or division. The problem then becomes one of fighting back to Headquarters, for it is the Headquarters' attorney who is on the rail to an executive position.

Being fielded out can be devastating in that many subs and divisions are located in those geographical areas of the nation or world that either no one in their right mind would visit or that no one of your race or creed would visit. In some instances, a division headquarters can arise overnight in a swamp and vanish just as quickly, so that the new in-house counsel finds himself following a peripatetic building.

You also have to remember that these in-house counsel are older lateral transfers who probably have families. Major corporations tend not to hire lawyers directly from law schools, but let them sweat out firm life for a minimum of two years. Moreover, the salary of an in-house attorney is well below going rate in a firm and, when the counsel is shifted to a sub or div, his salary will reflect the cost of living in that area.[2]

The training ground of a sub or div is the first contact the fledgling in-house counsel has with corporate politics. If he succeeds, he will build a power base, rise to general counsel - vice president of the sub or division, and then pull strings to get transferred back to Legal Headquarters.

We

The major difference the new attorney will perceive between working at a law firm and working in a corporation is that the politicking has a different flavor to it. Attorneys in firms think in terms of "I," as in "I will succeed." In-house counsel think in terms of "We," as in the corporation. The politicking is done within a corporate hierarchy composed of attorneys and executives, as opposed to just attorneys.

The sense of competition is, therefore, broader than in a firm. In-house counsel find themselves believing in the corporate goals, hoping that the corporation makes it while they make it within the corporation. There is more of a sense of commitment and of wanting to be recognized in terms of the tangibles.

For example, the largest corporations have security systems that require every employee to carry an identification card. The cards have the employees' photographs on them. The backdrop to each photograph and the employment code immediately tell everyone else in the company the level of the card holder. This is the American Express syndrome -- even with a famous name you won't be recognized without your card. If the corporation uses an alphabet scaling, so that an "A" means Chairman of the Board, and a colored backdrop, so that "blue" means an executive officer, a person walking into a corporate building and holding up a card containing both ele-

172

ments will have red carpets rolled before him and rose petals tossed in his path.

Moving up the ladder means gaining other signs of prestige, such as having the company limo pick you up each morning and drop you off each night. Or flying in the corporate helicopter to the corporate jet. Or staying in the corporate condominium when you visit subs or divisions in other cities. At financial institutions, such as banks, executives and in-house counsel have access to corporate restaurants run by three-star chefs.

A corporation will not fire an attorney who falls from grace, it will merely transfer him, at whatever age or seniority, to one of the outposts. The alternative is termed a golden handshake, which means if you do not want to live the rest of your life in the middle of a desert, you can take a year's salary and whatever other benefits have vested and leave.

Legal Work

Memo writing in a large corporation is not as redundant or prolonged as in a private firm and, in many instances, involves charts, graphs, and spreadsheets of one kind or another. Legal principles are explained in conference with executives on the basis of can this be done and, if so, what is the up-side and the down-side. If not, what is the maximum liability.

Legal memos are not as important as slide shows and general discussions. I remember bringing my first memo into a higher-up. It involved an analysis of a crucial issue where the amount of money at stake was, to me, monumental (about twelve billion dollars). He was sitting on his large leather recliner behind his large wood desk. I sat across from him and began to explain the memo. His eyes stopped blinking. He gazed at a spot to the right of my head with extreme intensity. In fact, he became catatonic for a minute or so, then slowly raised his right leg, all this while I was still explaining the memo, although with increasing rapidity. Finally, he let loose an astonishing fart, smiled, blinked, resettled on his chair, and said, "What were you

173

saying?"

Small corporations are not set up in quite the same manner. Typically, there will be one in-house counsel who had been an associate at a firm that brought the company public. The associate will join the corporation as General Counsel, Secretary and will soon receive the additional hat of Vice President.

He or she will tend to be young and sympatico with top management at the firm. His role will be to assuage the egos of the executives, give on-the-spot legal advice about everything from horse track racing, to copying someone else's advertisements, to arranging luncheons.

The nitty gritty work will be done by a Contracts Manager, a non-lawyer whose job is to coordinate the execution of contracts with the outside sales forces while ensuring that no one has changed the form contract the company has lived with for forty years (and which was originally drafted by the president's five year old daughter, currently serving as executive vice president).

Major work, and especially litigation, will be fielded out to the General Counsel's former law firm if the parting was on good terms. Eventually, however, the General Counsel will be caught up in the "We" mentality and will arrive at the same conclusion that the first corporation ever to hire in-house counsel discovered earlier: it is possible to pick up passed-over senior attorneys and/or top notch junior associates for a song. For example, assume you pay the new counsel between $18,000 and $30,000 to start; with benefits, the package "costs" the corporation between $30,000 and $50,000. If the new counsel comes up with one decision that nets $100,000, he has paid for himself. If he drafts and files UCC forms, he has paid for himself. If he handles copyright and trademark work, he has paid for himself. In short, the corporation will be saving a bundle.

Another aspect of this cost/benefit analysis is that part of a law firm's billings includes charges for overhead. In-house counsel, on the other hand, only incrementally increase the cost of overhead to a corporation. This is because a corporation can shop among states and counties to find the best combination of tax incentives and services which lower its initial investment in constructing a new building that contains thousands of cubicles (formed with movable partitions) in which it can seat hundreds of lawyers.

As it is, in-house counsel already perform a lot of work the major firms themselves are too embarrassed to handle. The primary example is the simple torts case -- someone trips on the ice in front of headquarters, an enraged daughter tosses the hair dryer into the bathtub while her mother is bathing, a coal miner chain smokes cigarettes and dies of cancer, or luggage is lost by an airline.

Law firms, for the most part, suppress their fear of expanded in-house staffing by corporations, with the result that one reads of firms shedding entire departments when a major client withdraws its work.

Private practice lawyers who can read the various handwritings on the wall (their or their firm's impending doom) inundate corporations with unsolicited resumes. Working in a corporation at least pulls some of the pieces together in that, instead of concentrating on overbilling dozens of clients, a lawyer can concentrate on working for a single client. Besides, corporate lawyers can introduce themselves at parties as "Esquire, executive vice president, *and* general counsel."

Fiascos

In-house counsel does not connote lifetime job security. Unlike a law firm, the politics involved are real -- lawyers must perform as both lawyers and businessmen, and the higher-ups they have to impress are usually not lawyers. These lawyers also have to be adept administrators.

But just as a law firm can fire entire departments or slews of associates if and when a major client leaves or a large case is settled, corporations can fire or give "early retirement" to a staff of in-house counsel. One bad year, even one bad day in the stock market, and the lawyers are among the first to go.

Lawyers are also expendable after their company is taken over by another company. (Why do you think corporations fight takeovers with the sword of God? Because in-house counsel have strongly advised the fight -- at least until they are assured positions in the new company.)

But the worst punishment for in-house counsel is when Headquarters decides to move from New York City to a place like Yoknapatawpha County.

Footnotes:

1. This brings up another distinction between a corporation and a law firm from a business point of view. Law firms rent space but, in many cities, the ultimate tax benefits and potential yields are not as good as owning the real estate. Since firms plan growth poorly, they often end up on different floors of a building or even in different buildings. Corporate counsel occupy space owned by the corporation or one of its subsidiaries.

2. Although the salaries are lower, the benefits are much better than at a law firm. A law firm, in my estimate, contributes approximately ten percent of an associate's income as additional benefits. Corporations average anywhere from fifty to seventy percent in packages covering health and life insurance, retirement, matching funds, stock option plans, and the like. It should also be noted that a senior in-house attorney will see a large salary jump and, if he makes it into the executive offices, can eventually achieve an income level much larger than that received by partners at firms.

CHAPTER ELEVEN

PUBLICATIONS, SEMINARS, AND BAR ASSOCIATIONS

Publications

Since the practice of law involves paper, a big business is printing things for lawyers to buy. This is an extremely lucrative field for a number of reasons.

First, law firms have money and can always get more by billing clients for the cost of publications.

Second, since lawyers charge outrageous fees for their services, they have no qualms about spending outrageous sums on books, journals, and law newspapers.

Third, some publications *have* to be owned by law firms. These include volumes of federal and state cases, statutes, rules, and regulations, and treatises.

Fourth, since being current is necessary to prevent embarrassment in court and at parties, law firms will subscribe to advance sheets (cases printed prior to binding in a volume) and to law journals (local and national newspapers that cater to the legal trade).

Fifth, since forms are the backbone of the legal practice, firms must own form books and purchase large quantities of unbound, fill-in-the-spaces forms.

One could actually go on and on listing reasons for purchasing publications -- and here the actual point is to drive the librarian crazy since he's the one who has to find a place for all those books, papers, and journals. But let's look at the topic from the point of view of the law publishing house.

State governments usually auction the right to be the official publisher of cases and statutes. By far, the publisher holding the most contracts as official publisher is West. West's volumes of federal cases have become the *de facto* official publication because judges send their opinions to West in exchange for volumes engraved with their names. West is also famous for its key numbers and headnotes which are supposed to synopsize and classify the major elements of a case.

West holds (and has held) a monopoly position in the case and statute publishing business. What is absurd about this position is that cases and statutes are in the public domain -- they cannot be copyrighted. But when one house has the "official" patina (and it's the "official" cite which has to be included in every memo and brief), lawyers will conclude that its is the edition they must have. Besides, these beige, gold, red, and black volumes of federal cases can be seen in *L.A. Law*, and clients will therefore expect to see the same volumes in a real law firm.

In the opinion of some, this monopoly position has led to inflated prices for public domain documents. But West might contend that one is paying not only for the official text, but also for the key numbers and headnotes (with reference numbers being incorporated into the public domain text) -- which are not public domain. This argument overlooks the fact that headnotes are primarily written by judges' law clerks, and that key numbers are purely subjective. Why does one have to wait for West to decide that an area of the law is an area of the law?

Another law publishing house -- Lawyer's Co-operative -- has attempted to compete with West by publishing its own unofficial and a limited number of official books of cases and statutes. Instead of key numbers, L.C. has emphasized the inclusion of annotations analyzing certain cases and bringing an area of law into perspective. These annotations are written by lawyers, which means very little -- the writers and editors at all law publishing houses are lawyers. The existence of a law publishing house competing in cases and statutes merely means that lawyers can append an "unofficial" cite after the "official" cite, thereby expanding a one page argument into a thirty page cite.

What is the value of a monopoly position, key numbers, headnotes, or annotations written by non-genetic lawyers? A monopoly position was supposed to ensure that an official edition would be available nationwide, which meant that when one went to a cite (the volume and page number of a case; the title and section number for a statute), everyone would have that volume available and would read the same thing. Key numbers and headnotes are supposed to speed the process of legal research. An annotation, regardless of who wrote it, is supposed to be a reliable source of legal trends and rules.

But today, none of those factors make any sense. Many courts and legislatures have computerized. Lawyers and laypeople alike should have direct, low-cost access to filed decisions. If the court's or legislature's computers cannot handle the demand, the database can be licensed out to numerous sources, such as Western Union.

Moreover, all cases and statutes are published whether or not they will ever be relevant to anyone. With statutes, one can always purchase a selected volume or two, since laws are grouped by titles designating the areas covered. But federal cases, for example, are grouped by volume according to the level of the court. Ninety percent of the cases in each volume will never be used by a purchaser, either because the court is not controlling or the decision is irrelevant.[1]

Instead of the official reports being divvied up by topic and circuit, the law publishers feed on the situation by providing specialty services. These do the dividing for the lawyer by topic (Tax, Labor, Bankruptcy).

All of these machinations about something otherwise simple creates a high-cost service industry, the cost of which is passed along to the clients. What has occurred is that free public domain material has become the bread and butter of publishers. Non-law publishing houses must drool whenever they think of the situation: the writers are free; the material is free; the target market is wealthy and feels compelled to purchase regardless of cost. The same cost structure is carried over into the computerized law searches provided by the two major law database providers (Westlaw, owned by West, and Lexis, owned by Mead Data). The cost of maintaining access, the cost of accessing (made difficult by cumbersome query programs, thereby spawning another service industry providing program overlays which use "plain" English), and the cost of obtaining copies (as of this writing, a firm cannot download the cases into its own computer) can be prohibitive -- but the searches are done anyway at the large firms, since the costs are passed on to the clients.

So lucrative is this computer-for-hire area that West has sued Mead Data to keep Lexis from going on-line with "official" pagination, which would mean that cases found (probably by accident) in the database could be cited without resort to a bound, West volume.

In the law, page numbers are a right to be protected through lengthy and expensive litigation.

Looseleaf Services

Another lucrative source of money for law publishers is the looseleaf service. A looseleaf is a hard binding of two covers held together by metal rods. Text is printed on paper which has holes that fit over the metal rods. When a firm first purchases a looseleaf book, it arrives in proper order with the text fitted over the holes and the top cover fastened on.

What happens thereafter is madness and mayhem. One to fifteen times a year, the book is "updated." An update might be one page, or it might be a thousand pages. The firm is charged for each update -- having the option, of course, to return the update and not be charged, which would supposedly make the entire book useless.

So the firm pays and a person already driven mindless has to unfasten the cover of the book, remove the pages from the rods, carefully replace each old page with an update page, put the pages back into the binder, replace the top cover, and then scream.

The incentive behind looseleaf services is similar to that in computer software. You buy Version 1.01. A month later, you can receive Version 1.01a for free. But from then on, you can be hit with an update charge. Version 1.01, which was probably sold at a substantial discount and seemed like a tremendous bargain, suddenly becomes one of a series of more and more expensive albatrosses, but you are psychologically caught in the process of not wanting to be out-of-date. You need to protect your original investment.

For example, you buy the "current" volume for seventy to a hundred and twenty dollars. You spend between seventy and two hundred dollars a year on updates. Yet you have no idea as to the value of the updates,[2] except that everyone says that the law "changes."

What no one seems to realize is that law publishers have the same time lags as regular publishing houses. On the average, there is a one year delay from when an author submits an update to when it is finally mailed out to a subscriber. During that time, cases can be overruled, statutes passed, and nuclear war declared.

From the law publisher's point of view, looseleafs are better than selling a bound book because the latter are revised at most once a year. A bound book is then either replaced with a new edition, or the update is an inexpensive pocket supplement. But with a looseleaf service, there is the possibility of having a firm purchase the equivalent of two to ten books a year, even though the pages fit into the one volume.

Treatises

Articles and books in the law follow the same road as publishing in general: use a form, get it out. Many of these publications are just rewrites of in-house and advisory memoranda originally written by associates and published under the partner's byline.

Some are just rewrites of a statute -- for example, the complete book on the Bankruptcy Code that merely rephrases each section of the Code and then reprints the Code as an appendix.

Some are rewrites of major treatises or older articles. Some are just descriptive of a new case. Some are just outright stolen, as where an associate attempting a lateral transfer tries to impress the interviewer with his insight into a particular area and explains it in such detail that the interviewer can rapidly turn it into lucrative print.

The law publishers are to blame for much of this. Like any publisher, they want to fill their lists. Unlike other publishers, they are often forced to contract with lawyers based upon geography. Believe it or not, most of the complaints a law publishing house receives have to do with whether enough authors are from the complaining lawyer's state!

Newsletters

Another scam involves newsletters. It is an extremely profitable business. Sure there are start-up costs, but newsletters sell in the range of $175 to $300 a year (and sometimes much more). If you send out direct mail ads to 100,000 attorneys and get an initial response of three percent -- 3,000 -- and half of those remain as paid subscribers -- 1,500 -- you are grossing in the range of a quarter of a million dollars a year.

A newsletter is either eight or sixteen pages long, printed on relatively cheap paper, and having at most a two-color cover. It is mailed out at a bulk rate. The contributors are not paid because there is no need to -- lawyers are always looking for outlets for their "articles" in the hope of attracting clients or referrals. In short, net profits are, at a minimum, fifty percent of gross receipts.

What is contained in these newsletters? Not much. Recent cases are synopsized. Someone has an article on "recent trends." Someone else has a chatty article on a personal experience, such as coping with or getting clients. The last page of each issue is set aside as a subscription form.

Sales

The sale of sets, books, looseleafs, and other services is through direct mail, space ads, and promotion by the author through writing monthly columns or giving seminars.

Direct mail is simple enough for everyone: rent a list from the bar associations and send out copy. As soon as a lawyer passes the bar exam, he or she will be on a mailing list.

Space ads and promotions are generally related. The New York Law Journal is a good example of this mix and match. On the front page, one will find the monthly articles written by "experts" in the field. On the third page, one will often find a quarter page or larger space ad promoting that same expert's book or newsletter, which will just happen to be published by the New York Law Journal's publishing arm. Then, on the next page, there will be a similar space ad promoting a seminar (run by another subsidiary of the Journal) on that topic, which seminar is to be led by that same expert and the book for which will be that expert's book, published by the arm of the newspaper that prints the article that sells the ...

Seminars

Law seminars are supposed to be educational experiences which give those attending an extensive grounding in the selected area of law. The lawyers teaching at the seminar are supposed to be experts in their fields. Attending seminars is promoted by bar associations as a means for keeping up-to-date with legal trends (much as attending medical seminars is promoted by the American Medical Association).

In reality, seminars are a way to get out of the firm for one to four days. A quality seminar will be held out of the city or country. The cost of a seminar can therefore range from four hundred to three thousand dollars. At the lower cost, one can expect breakfast, coffee, soda, and a paperback book. At the high end, one will return with a sun tan, fifteen rolls of exposed film, and some anecdotes about sexual life abroad.

The learning value of these seminars is nil. The experts use phrases like: "As I write in my book .....," "According to a recent article printed in my newsletter ...," and "That's a complicated area

I don't think we have time to explore here, but if you would look at chapter four of my looseleaf ..." Of course, all of those books and article reprints are either included in the cost of the seminar or available for sale during the coffee break.

Moreover, the same people always run the same seminars on the same topics. Only in a few cases have they learned any Siskel and Ebert tactics; snores are usually rampant after the first fifteen minutes.

In fact, the high point of these seminars seems to be when that one attractive woman walks down the aisle to her seat, or walks up the aisle to get coffee. Then all heads (male, from desire; female, to check out why *she's* getting attention) move, first left to right, then right to left. If the ceiling is mirrored, all heads crane backward.

Bar Associations

Bar associations are included in this chapter because they offer: magazines, newsletters, books, and seminars. These associations like to pretend that they do more than that, compiling "reports" on various local, regional, and national topics, putting together codes of "ethics," and recommending lawyers for judgeships. But those matters are all handled by committees, and membership in committees depends upon whom you know who knows the chairman of the committee.

But for your dues (which increase dramatically the longer you're out of law school), you receive publications full of useless articles by committee chairpeople and a bit of local gossip by freelancers.

Other than these glossies, bar associations are good for only two other aspects of getting by: "gold" credit cards from strangely named banks, and group insurance.

Publications, Seminars, and Bar Associations

Footnotes:

1. Most cases involve criminal law, the only value of which to law firms is that late at night, the reading aloud of rape decisions by haggard associates seems to maintain legal sanity.
2. Law books are not read by lawyers until absolutely necessary. When a particular issue arises, an associate or paralegal will ask the librarian where to look. The librarian will point to a book. The associate or paralegal will glance at the index and turn only to the page cited under the appropriate heading. The value of an updated page in a looseleaf service is more likely than not never to be known.

CHAPTER TWELVE

CLIENTS

There are good clients and bad clients. A good client is someone who pays and pays and pays without objection, whether the legal services are necessary, valid, or valuable. A bad client questions bills and does not pay.

Good Clients

Good clients are usually easy to find for large firms with impressive letterheads. They are the overweight bodies of corporate presidents tanning on the same shores partners will then start tanning at.[1] They are the relations of associates and partners who feel they should give their work to the firm. They are the beneficiaries of trust funds, where the funds are being handled by the firm (in other words, a conflict of interest situation frequently overlooked by firms). They are former college classmates. They are the in-house counsel of corporations who field out work to firms from which the counsel came or to which the lawyer would like to go.

The relationship of a firm with one of the above clients is simply stated: We are family. The phrase might not be sung, but it is latent in the air as the client enters the lobby and the partner comes in, rubbing his hands together, giving an effusive greeting and patting the old fellow on the back as he is led to a conference room for a preliminary discussion prior to lunch. Lawyer and president play tennis and golf at the same club; they live in similar neighborhoods; they drive the same cars; their children attend the same private schools; their wives have their hair permed at the same parlor. Just as a son or daughter will hurriedly put out the photographs of the in-

HOW CLIENTS ARE MADE; WHY FRANCHISES
ADVERTISE AS THEY DO

The meek of the earth shall never inherit it; they will instead wake up one morning being hauled off to prison. It is that fear which some of the franchises play on in advertisements showing people who look just like us using their last dime to place a call to a lawyer.

The get-me-out-of-here syndrome does have some basis in fact. The following is an edited version of a real case, reported as Orndorff v. De Nooyer, 117 AD2d 365 (3d Dep't 1986).

"As a result of an accident ... plaintiff left his car ... for repairs at an auto body shop of defendant De Nooyer Chevrolet, Inc. (De Nooyer). This commenced a chain of events which evolved into a consumer's nightmare.

"... De Nooyer agreed to repair all of the damage ... for ... $2,850... Plaintiff was also assured that the work to be performed would be completed [within three months].

"[Months later], plaintiff ... went out to De Nooyer to check on the status of his car. Plaintiff proceeded to the storage area where his car was kept, only to find it literally filled with garbage ...

"[After numerous promises by De Nooyer, which went unfulfilled for almost two years], plaintiff ventured out to the back storage lot to ascertain whether his car was still on the premises. At this point in time, plaintiff decided to start up his car and drive it to another service station for repairs. Plaintiff dropped the car off at a Sunoco station, went back to his office and allegedly attempted to contact [De Nooyer] to inform [it] of his actions, but was unable to reach [it]. Plaintiff picked up the car later that evening from the Sunoco station, drove it to his home and left it in his garage over the weekend.

"... [De Nooyer] contacted the police department ... [and] executed a stolen car report. As a postscript to that report ... [it]

---

affixed the following: "Car may be in possession of owner; owner possibly took car and did not pay $4000 bill." ...

"At approximately 12:56 A.M. on Wednesday ... plaintiff was stopped by a ... police car ... Plaintiff ... was required to follow [the police] to the Town's police station. ... Upon his arrival at the Town's police station, plaintiff was given the *Miranda* warnings, was arrested and signed a voluntary statement about the incident. ... [P]laintiff asserted: "I had no intention in *not* paying the bill. I only wanted my car back..." After his arrest, plaintiff was subsequently fingerprinted and had mug shots taken. Plaintiff was then handcuffed to another suspect and transported ... for arraignment. Plaintiff was then transferred to ... Jail where he was subjected to a full body search. He was then held overnight ...

" ...[N]o probable causes for plaintiff's arrest existed ... Here, plaintiff was shown to be an individual with no prior criminal record, a Major in the Air Force Reserves and a respected employee of a large corporation. As a result of defendants' actions, plaintiff was arrested, handcuffed, fingerprinted, photographed, forced to undergo a strip search and held in custody... In addition, plaintiff was subjected to ridicule and embarrassment due to the publication in the local newspaper of his prosecution for stealing a car. ..."

Moral: Never drive your own car.

---

laws prior to their arrival, the partner will have a paralegal retrieve the volumes of bound corporate documents and set them up where the client will notice them. Bills are sent once a month with two typed lines: one for professional services rendered; the other for disbursements. Bills are paid on the fifteenth of every month.

Sometimes, a partner does not even have to go overboard with friendliness and shows of personal concern. In some instances, a client will feel obligated to continue using the partner and the firm solely because a relationship exists. It is like a patient/doctor rela-

WHAT A CLIENT SHOULD DO
(Regardless of Size)

FINDING A LAWYER/LAW FIRM

Call local bar associations to see if they keep lists by specialty.
Research educational credentials of a partner using Martindale Hubbell, *Who's Who*'s, and college and university alumni books.

Referrals from friends -- but check out as above anyway.

Call the firm and request a free conference. Use the conference wisely, as by presenting a legal problem and seeing how the firm would handle it. How many partners, associates, and paralegals would be assigned to any particular case? What would they be billed out at? What retainers are required, particularly for litigation services? Will the firm place a cap on certain matters? Ask to see a typical bill, and then ask to see what would be included on an itemized bill.

Interview a number of firms and lawyers.

HANDLING THE LAWYERS/LAW FIRMS

Immediately take the attitude that the firm is looking for billings and that although everyone smiles at you, you really only look like a dollar sign.

When a matter arises, do not rush over to the firm. Collect the relevant documents, have them copied, and have your secretary compile a chronology. Draft a brief history of the matter, what the problem is, and the solutions you believe are viable. Send these over to the firm and ask them to only review the matter, without additional research, and to call you with an initial response. The partner is supposed to have experience; if the call back is a whiny declaration the tons of research must be done by a variety of associates, threaten to take the matter elsewhere.

For each matter, have the firm send you a statement that there is no conflict of interest but, if one develops, then the firm will ensure (for free) that you will have the time to select another attorney. The firm's final bill should reflect a discount equivalent to what it cost you to find the new firm.

In litigation matters, have the firm send you a statement that the suit to be filed on your behalf is not frivolous but, if it is, the firm will swallow the costs, fees, and penalties.

State in advance that in no event are lawyers to have lunches or dinners for the "benefit" of you or your company. If your company is nearby, say that you will provide catered meals for anyone actually working through a meal; and that your car service will provide transportation for lawyers who work past eight or nine o'clock at night.

If you are computerized, state that you will assist in computerized law searches, and want to approve all queries that are to be made. If a lawyer feels it is essential to make an inquiry late at night because of a rush job, state that you want print-outs of the queries made.

If the firm is going to bill you for word processing and secretarial services, state that you want the originals of all documents so that you can track how many drafts something had to go through.

Ask for copies or originals of all documents generated by the firm.

If more than one partner is going to work on a case, ask for the credentials and billing rates of the other partners and associates who will be assigned to the matter, along with an explanation as to the use each will be put to.

Never, never give original documents to the law firm. Always give clear xeroxes. If a firm requires a number of copies of any document for use as an exhibit or for discovery, provide the copies yourself.

WHAT THE INDIVIDUAL CLIENT SHOULD DO
(Regardless of Height)

Never, ever go to a lawyer who advertises on match boxes, in subways, or buses.

Approach franchises with caution, asking not only for the credentials of the lawyer who will be handling your case, the billed rate, and the estimated cost (those flat fees mean nothing; they are generally come-on's), but what happens, for example, if the matter becomes too large or complex for that lawyer.

Remember that when a lawyer or firm advertises that it will take your medical malpractice or injury case for "free," that what is meant is a contingency fee agreement. These agreements are usually not regulated. You may discover that you will be responsible for certain charges, such as filing fees, xeroxing, messengers, and trips to the site of the accident -- whether or not money to cover those items is won from the opposing party. You may find that the firm will ask for fifty or more percent of the damages awarded. You may also discover that your lawyer has negotiated a settlement that is structured to pay most or all of the award up-front, even though a structured award, such as an annuity, might benefit you more -- the lawyer's incentive is to get as much as possible up-front so that he can claim his entire percentage. Alternatively, a well-structured contingency fee arrangement could help you -- the lawyer, after all, is taking a risk with the case and will be spending money on research, time in court, and the hiring of expert witnesses.

Try for binding mediation, arbitration, or small claims' court (by judge or arbitrator, preferably the latter) as much as possible. These services are somewhat informal, cost very little, and can resolve most issues satisfactorily. The most beneficial time for looking into mediation: divorce without children, or where there is no issue as to custody. Divorces are emotionally charged to begin with; once lawyers become involved, those emotions will be manipulated to the point of explosive hatred, thereby increasing fees. There is no such thing as a "simple fifty dollar" divorce when two lawyers become involved. Nor should the two spouses have the same lawyer simulate mediation for them. At most, each spouse can consult his or her own lawyer of choice for a description of legal rights -- but again, that hook of rising emotions will probably come into play. It is safer to buy a book on divorce rights from a law school bookstore; then go to mediation with your list of demands.

tionship. I needed a doctor; I found a doctor in the yellow pages; I came to the doctor; he treated me, perhaps not well, but I survived; I will continue seeing that doctor. This dependency seems to be based on fear: the doctor might reject me as a patient, and then I will have to start all over again. And the longer the relationship continues, the more the fear evolves, until the client becomes absolutely nerve-wracked at the thought that he might be considered a bad patient at some point. The doctor has all the records; the doctor knows the case history; the doctor knows the cures. So it is with some clients and their lawyers.

Sometimes, a good client becomes a very, very bad client, as where there is a corporate shift and the new in-house counsel insists upon itemized bills. But that is not as bad as where the client actually changes law firms, whether by following a partner or because of whim. When a large, institutional client leaves a large, institutional law firm, it can practically destroy the firm. It certainly forces the partners to fire as many associates as they can find.

What makes a good client leave a large firm (other than through following a transfer by a beloved partner)? The realization that the firm has not done anything to deserve all that money.

Bad Clients

From a firm's point of view, a bad client is one who does not pay on time while questioning everything on the bill (not that firms won't bill for questions about bills).

Bad clients come in all shapes and sizes. One kind abuses the services of the firm, whether by calling at all hours to see if their matters are being given priority, or by insisting that the free conference is still continuing even though the matter has since been staffed and moved ahead, or by bursting into the firm without an appointment and screaming in the lobby that their friend had an eight page complaint filed and they were given only a six page complaint for the same price.

Another bad client is the corporation which pays promptly while a matter is being litigated or negotiated but, once the matter is settled, the final bill always seems to be lost in the mail -- until a new matter arises.

The worst client is the one who not only doesn't pay, but also relegates the care of his entire life to the lawyer and firm. These clients want advice on everything under the sun and would actually be better served hiring away a partner's secretary.

Law Plans

In 1987, press releases panted with announcements about law plans. Anyone, for a small annual fee, could sign up. Some companies started including the plans as part of the benefit package.

These plans strike me as being modeled after the usual dental plan -- you are permitted one cleaning, one set of x-rays, two fillings, and maybe a cap per year, so long as the total cost does not pass an established ceiling. If you pass the ceiling or require major work, you are on your own.

Joining a plan typically means that you receive one simple will and one simple divorce. In other words, the same two matters you could do on your own if you wanted. But using the plan means going into the lawyer's office. You wait for an hour, are called in, go over the will or divorce (there goes the one free hour of consultation), the lawyer nods, clasps his hands together, and says, "Have you thought of this angle? That angle? And what if this happens? Are you *sure*?" Of course you're not sure. The matter suddenly becomes "complex," which means it is outside of the plan and you will be billed for services rendered.

Another aspect of these plans similar to medical plans is that you must select your law "clinic" from a booklet of "providers." What if you discover, too late, that these fellows have the same mentality as anyone else working for a franchise?

Rights Against Lawyers

If you are paid up, you own all documents you provided to the lawyer and which the lawyer prepared on your behalf. (The ownership to the lawyer's work product should include copyrights and the ability to prevent the lawyer from incorporating his work into the work done for other clients, but lawyers will successfully argue otherwise. Nonetheless, you have a right to everything in your file.) Get the documents.

You can also sue a lawyer for malpractice. In the typical case, this is not easy to win, since you have to prove that if the lawyer had acted properly, you would have won a certain amount of money. But there are new kinds of malpractice opening up all the time.

One involves suing a lawyer who advised a client, and the result of that advice and any ensuing actions foreseeably impacted on you. In this group, one might find a beneficiary of a trust suing the lawyer who set up the trust or who is acting as a trustee, even though the lawyer was representing the person establishing the trust. Or, the lawyer who drafts a will later held to be invalid, where you were to have been the heir. Or, the law firm that advises an investment manager, knowing that the manager intended to perform illegal acts, and you are a client of the manager.

Another kind of malpractice involves foreseeable conflict of interest. Lawyers will give up a case just about when Hell freezes over, which means that conflicts are often memo'd away. But if the opposing party brings up the issue and the judge agrees, you can be left holding the bag, without a lawyer. The law firm should not bill you, since you will have to find another lawyer and start all over.

Frivolous suits are another possibility. More and more, rules are being passed which provide for the assessment of a penalty against a lawyer and/or a client for filing a civil lawsuit which is frivolous. If you go to a lawyer and discuss a matter fully and honestly, and the lawyer says, Yes, there is a valid case here, let's sue, give me a five thousand dollar retainer, the least a lawyer can do is to sign an agreement saying that he (or his firm) will pay for any penalties.

Footnotes:

1. Just as there are books listing nude beaches (illustrated), there are books listing corporate vacation spots. Lawyers purchase both types.

CHAPTER THIRTEEN

JUDGES

Becoming A Judge

Judges are lawyers. Lawyers want to be federal judges. A judge wants to be chief or presiding judge. A chief judge wants to be at the appellate level. An appellate level judge wants to be on the Supreme Court. A Supreme Court Justice wants to write Majority Opinions overruling cases that he never understood in law school.

Those who don't become appellate level or Supreme Court judges want to return to private practice as a name member of a prestige firm and make a bundle.

Becoming a judge has nothing to do with merit but instead with political contacts and calling favors due. Judges spend half their time politicking and the other half drinking in chambers while complaining loudly to the wall that they deserve double the salary they are receiving. This is not to say that all judges are bad, but only that most judges are merely lawyers and do not rise above the bluffery and bickering that lawyers carry around in their lit. bags.

After all, judgeships are based upon law firm practice: judges are the partners, and the legal work is fielded out to judicial clerks. Thus, as in real life, judges are known to get drunk (some fall off their benches, others get drunk at parties); known to womanize (particularly with law secretaries and jurors, but sometimes with defendants in criminal cases); known to miss legal points completely while sitting on the bench; and known to nap daily after lunch.

The appellate process is not based on making sure that the law is served, but on the possibility that an appellant might come across a sober judge without sex on his mind who might give a relatively unbiased opinion on a legal issue. But most litigants do not appeal because $50,000 to $500,000 is an awful lot to pay for the possibility

---

ON SALARIES AND MERIT

The great debate has centered on this: Judges should be paid as much as partners in law firms because that way better lawyers will be attracted to the judiciary.

The assumption is that the income of partners is based upon merit, and paying the same amounts to judges will bring in lawyers who also merit that kind of money.

But partners are not paid based upon merit. A partner can get his share for any number of reasons. He might be good at bringing in clients, while being incompetent in the actual practice of law. He might be the senior name partner on the letterhead, who receives his share based upon being senile. He might be a good bluffer. He might be the son-in-law of someone Famous. He might be adept at overbilling clients, as by fielding out work of little meaning or value to a dozen associates who create a job of massive proportions.

The ignored issue is whether the judge is a good judge. How does government attract a "good" judge? No one knows whether it is the money which compels a lawyer to try for a judgeship; there are, after all, other perks.

---

of finding a sober needle in the haystack. And, if you do go all the way up to the Supreme Court, yours might be that one case for which the majority of Justices has been waiting all their lives to pounce on for the purpose of overruling those decisions they never understood. And you were the fool who paid through the nose to give them that chance!

To look a little more closely at the politicking process, note that at the appellate level, there are panels of judges. Assume a chief judge (hereinafter, "CJ") and another senior judge. We will also assume a Democratic administration and that the CJ and the senior judge are both Democrats. Each has the same political power; each has thrown or attended parties for the administration; each has the same or similar ethnic background. Assume that a slot will be opening up at the next higher appellate level (e.g., the Supreme Court of the state or the federal appeals court). It is generally considered in the legal community that either the CJ or the senior judge will be nominated in the selection process for the higher seat.

Since I have purposely painted a picture of all things being equal, the issue for our judges is how are they going to distinguish themselves in the eyes of the administration? The answer is in their opinions. Thus, the concept of majority and minority opinions. Just for the heck of it, I once followed an exchange of decisions in the exact context just described. The CJ and the senior judge always ended up on opposite sides of a decision, not because they believed in the legal justice of what they were writing (oftentimes, they would be contradicting their own earlier decisions), but because they wanted to discredit their opponent for the better judgeship.

If you think that politics plays no role in judgeships, a good contemporary example is the Bankruptcy Court. Under the old Bankruptcy Act, those persons who presided over bankruptcy proceedings were termed "referees" and instead of wearing judicial robes, they wore white and black striped silk shirts.[1] Under the new Bankruptcy Code, they were elevated to the position of "judges," but they were not real judges in the sense of the Constitution. They were semi-judges.[2]

The problem with semi-judges is that they do not have the power to hear certain types of proceedings heard by real judges. The obvious solution is to make the semi-judges real judges, but real judges don't want to have their power diluted by having hundreds of new judges hanging around chambers, and Congressmen don't want presidents of a different political persuasion appointing hundreds of new real judges who believe in the wrong political idea of justice.

The United States Supreme Court, being composed of *real* judges, held that the semi-judges could not constitutionally hear those proceedings that must be heard by real judges and tossed the ball into the Congressional court. The Congress, with its usual alacrity, has tried to forget the problem in the hope that everyone else will forget about it. A solution will eventually be worked out -- a political solution.

Speaking of the Supreme Court, the highest court in the land with the largest marble building, the most polished solid wood, the most staff, and the best cafeteria, how does one get appointed? Morality? Intellectual abilities?

Presidents are court packers. Since openings on the Supreme Court do not usually occur during a presidential term, presidents devote their energies to the lower federal courts. Since these lower courts set most of the legal standards for their jurisdictions, and since these federal judges serve for life, packing in those who subscribe to a president's ideological incoherency (right-wing; left-wing; strict constructionist; anti-constructionist) can yield a couple of decades of political decision-making across the nation. Long after a president has pled *nolo contendere* and fled to his mansion, these judges can bang gavels and declare, No abortions, No homosexuality, No films or writings that offend me.

Lower court nominees are not subject to intense scrutiny with the exception of appointments to the appellate courts in important circuits, such as the Second, D.C., and Ninth. But even there, any controversy will quickly blow over.

Supreme Court nominees, however, are subject to scrutiny, which would normally lead one to believe that presidents would probe the nation for great legal minds. But presidents don't; they look for those who have expressed views similar to theirs. A lawyer's belief in a president's vision is sufficient for any president to pronounce the lawyer morally fit -- even though a president's vision is political and not based on moral rights or wrongs. This premise again points out the popular confusion with issues by entertaining three declarations, such as "Abortions are politically impermissible," "Abortions are legally wrong," and "Abortions are morally wrong." On an absolute level, if the polis is based on individual rights, then there is no political right to prevent a woman from making a personal decision which affects no one else as much as it affects her. Abortions can be legislated as legally wrong or dangerous (as by withholding funds or information), but that doesn't mean that the results will have a positive impact on the public; women either will have more children they don't want, or they will have illegal abortions. Besides, if the polis is based on individual rights, and if there is room within a constitution to find a right to have an abortion, then that the legislation has passed does not mean that the law is valid (but until it is found invalid, a lot of people will suffer). The moral issue is absurd because that inevitably boils down to groups of people screaming at each other that God has spoken to them and no one else. Ultimately, these "visions" of presidents, joined by those wanting to be on the Supreme Court, are only euphemisms for saying: I want to ensure that people live and act the way I do for even if what they do is only a superficial obedience, the nation will at least *look* the way I want it to.

Sometimes, the president's vision is even simpler -- find me someone who can be told how to think, but whose appointment will also get me additional votes. Taking a look at two presidents and what they did, Nixon nominated to the High Court one Clement F. Haynsworth, Jr., the chief judge of the South Carolina court of appeals. Nixon was planning for the 1972 presidential campaign and wanted a Southerner so that he could declare that his selection showed how nice he was to the South. Unfortunately, it turned out that Haynsworth had a stock portfolio and had sat on cases which affected the value of the portfolio. So Nixon nominated Harrold Carswell, a fellow from Florida who had recently been appointed to the federal court of appeals. It turned out that Carswell was not what one would call a thinker. Before the Senate turned him down, Senator Roman Hruska of Nebraska shouted: "There are a lot of mediocre judges and people and lawyers. Aren't they entitled to a little representation ...?"

Ronald Reagan's fiascos were not based on a Southern strategy of vote-getting, but on wanting someone who had a shared vision (of overturning a number of Supreme Court decisions giving too many rights to people). I recently read an article written by an important lawyer who had endorsed Bork for his current judgeship in the D.C. Court of Appeals, one of three most crucial federal judgeships in the country. The lawyer was trying to explain why he had said it was all right for Bork to have that judgeship without opposition, when he could in no manner support Bork for the Supreme Court.

I think what he was saying was this: It is all right to support (or not oppose) the appointment of a narrow-minded, socially imperceptive, and pig-headed lawyer to a court where he has some power, but can always be overruled. The U.S. Supreme Court, however, cannot always be overruled, particularly on questions involving an interpretation of Constitutional rights, and Bork's appointment could swing the Court the wrong way, since Reagan had already been permitted to appoint a number of narrow-minded, socially imperceptive, and pig-headed lawyers to it.

In any event, Bork's outrageous righteousness was too much for the Senate to stomach and he toddled off to make money on the lecture circuit. As Nixon had done, Reagan then turned to a lawyer who had served on the bench for only a short time. Senator Orrin Hatch (Utah) proclaimed, "I do not expect Judge Ginsburg to have any controversy at all." The FBI interviewed 140 people who knew Ginsburg or of him; the Senate Judiciary Committee apparently neglected to review Ginsburg's questionnaire, filled out in 1986 when he was nominated to the federal appellate bench, and in which he listed areas of possible conflict of interest. The Reagan administration started harping on how the new nominee was a Jew (presumably on the stereotypical assumption that most lawyers are Jewish and can control endorsements).

What was wrong with Ginsburg? Possible conflicts of interest. Little courtroom experience. Few written decisions. And -- the earlier use of marijuana.[3]

At the state levels, judges are either appointed or elected, with their terms ranging upward from one year. As with federal courts, if Republicans are in power, Republican judges are promoted; if the Democrats are in power, Democratic judges are promoted. Lawyers wanting to be judges therefore participate actively in local and regional political groups. Once appointed or elected, a judge will

JUDGES AND SEX

Like any lawyer, judges often spend their days doing any of the following: eating; talking about eating; sleeping; placing bets on horses; chatting with lawyers about their cases; drinking; going to movies. But what judges really like doing is getting under the skin of women. A judge, for example, might call bench conferences just so that he can say something snide to a female attorney, such as, You aren't up to snuff today, Hortense. Period bothering you?

But what judges like even more is hiring female law clerks or law secretaries (attorneys who do the research and writing) and getting them into bed. This is often not difficult, since attorneys have terrible father complexes, and a judge symbolizes the dark father of us all, dressed in black robes and dispensing justice from a high bench.

If it happens that the judge falls in love with his clerk, then things work out fine. The clerk stops working, they become engaged, they marry.

More often, the judge is already married and merely wants sex with obedience. He believes himself to be the father complex and, having psychologically bullied the clerk into bedding with him, he cannot bear to think of her leaving him. In two instances reported during just the past few months, the judges berated their clerks, called their boyfriends and made threatening remarks, camped outside of their clerks' apartment buildings, held their breath, and jumped up and down.

Judges also have a great vantage point for looking down blouses. Criminal and civil court judges are renowned for cruising prospective jurors and often making suggestive comments. (But then, there are some repeat jurors who are renowned for coming on to lawyers, much as some nurses come on to doctors.)

lobby even more actively, attending political meetings, giving political speeches, and putting down competing judges. The goal of a judge is to become another kind of judge. If there is an easily obtained opening on, say, the lower Criminal bench, the lawyer will take that. He will then cultivate the administration, his political power brokers, and the mayor or governor. When there is an opening on the Civil bench, he will be switched over. Then he will run for the elective judgeship and reach one of the higher state courts. On a higher state court bench, he will marshall his political forces so that he will be named Chief Judge when that spot is vacated. He will then forge a court philosophy which, in his opinion, will attract the attention of right-minded politicians, so that at the next opening on the state's highest appeals' court, or in the federal judiciary, he will be the one nominated and appointed.

A Typical Day

At the lower levels of practice, one confronts judges who may have little interest in what they are doing, perhaps because they have not reached the stage in their tenure where political steam builds up. Take a motion for injunctive relief.

What happens is that plaintiff brings a document termed a Temporary Restraining Order (TRO) to the judge's chambers for signature, without notice to the defendant. Presumably, the plaintiff must make a showing in chambers to get the TRO signed, since the TRO will have a litany of things the defendant can or cannot do, including breathing and taking his children to a picnic in another state. Judges typically riffle through the pages with an intent look on their faces, and then sign. One judge asked me to get his tobacco pouch and then signed. Another judge crossed out some lines and added some others. (Note: the prepared attorney will add superfluous lines to his TRO and will also repeat the same sentences in different paragraphs, foreseeing that a judge will want to cross out something to show that he has read the papers.)

One reason judges frequently sign TRO's without much ado is

that a TRO is quickly followed by a hearing. Once signed, an order to show cause is served on defendant's attorney, always on a Friday, and always returnable on a Monday morning so that defendant's attorneys can work around the clock all weekend.

Monday morning rolls around and everyone goes to court. A state courthouse is always the ugly, dirty, unkempt square building next to the clean, modern, shiny federal courthouse. The heater never works, the windows won't open, and Mr. Giggle is there.

Mr. Giggle is the crazy guy with buttons all over his suit. He carries two plastic bags filled with his life's belongings and is inevitably in court suing someone *pro se*, handing in papers written on used napkins found in wastepaper baskets.

Mr. Clerk is there, too. Mr. Clerk is the pot-bellied, balding fellow in the blue polyester suit sitting behind the table set in front of the judge's bench. He is responsible for accepting submissions, calling the calendar, and keeping general order in the courtroom. He is not a man to tangle with. And, if you do tangle with him, your papers will be lost (no big deal, since they'll be lost eventually anyway), your case will not appear on the calendar, and you will get hemorrhoids.

In the courtroom are the attorneys. There are the real estate attorneys on retainer to large real estate firms. They are dressed in paisley polyester suits, with brown ties, pink socks, and black shoes. They are reading the horse racing section of the local newspaper. There might be a few pinstripes there, hunched over their glossy litigation bags. There might be some clients, checking up on things. Attorneys meander up and down the aisles calling out the names of their adversaries for the service of papers.

The first call begins and Mr. Clerk goes through his calendar. Attorneys rush up, yelling out things like, "Submit plaintiff's memorandum of law on motion for dismissal." Others shout out, "Plaintiff present, ready to argue." Mr. Clerk then goes through a quick second calendar call, and then recesses so that the judge can smoke a cigarette in chambers.

It is only at the tail end of the session that the oral arguments are heard. In one case I was present at, the judge was, unfortunately, sound asleep. Not that that matters much anyway, since most arguments are made to a judge's law clerk. It is the law clerk who has read the papers if anyone has and who may still be awake. After the argument, the clerk will gently awaken the judge and whisper the decision in the judge's ear.

The five or ten minute oral argument before a judge is the height of litigation practice at large firms. Most associates do not even get a chance to perform that until they have been "litigating" for five or six years. As far as trials go, I have met one or two litigation partners at large firms who have done trials, but most such partners, upon hearing the word trial, hit the floor. The usual course of litigation is a flurry of papers, perhaps some depositions, maybe one oral argument, and then settlement.

A tip for clients: use small, hungry firms where the litigators pride themselves on going to trial. Since your opponent will be represented by a large firm, a more favorable settlement can be reached where the opposing litigation partner does not know how to select a jury.

Practice in a Bankruptcy Court is somewhere between state and federal practice. Bankruptcy Courts, as pointed out above, have never been considered "real" courts and although the courts are in nice federal buildings, the courtrooms tend to be somewhat shoddy.

The worst bankruptcy practice entails the individual bankruptcies brought on to prevent a state foreclosure proceeding instituted by a bank. These Chapter 13's are usually heard first in the morning. The courtroom will be filled with minority group families where the husband has fled, the wife is sick, the children are sick, and none of them understood what they were doing when they took out the note and mortgage on their shabby home.[4] The attorney representing the bank will be from a major firm and will be going up against an attorney who looks like his clients and who is handling hundreds of those cases. The genetic attorney will invariably succeed in having the case tossed out and the family evicted and will sleep the sleep of the righteous.

"Real" federal court is the court of choice. Lawyers get to sit on plush high-backed chairs before solid wood tables. Arguments are made from beautiful podiums. The courtroom is large and smells expensive. The judges have silvery hair and sit elevated well above everyone else.

All of this is, of course, only part of the show. If you have a father complex, courts are the place to live it out. Most lawyers are terrible in court. They tremble, they don't speak loudly enough, they lose their train of thought, and sometimes they cry. Witnesses are no better and, in fact, run a high risk of having a heart attack on the stand.

Judges who remain awake play on these fears and, if they sense a lack of fear, they will attempt to promote the emotion. Judges, after all, can interrupt whenever they wish and say whatever they wish. One trick, for example, is to play the hypothetical game learned during law school, as where a judge changes his questions midstream to discombobulate the attorney.

Another trick is for a judge to interrupt an attorney and "summarize" what the attorney has just said in a manner that will fit in better with the judge's perception of the case. If the attorney corrects the judge's interpretation, the judge will get back later on by overruling that attorney's objections.

At the appellate level, an attorney may find himself battered with a string of questions tossed at him from a panel of judges who are reading from the lists prepared by their law clerks. The questions are often off-the-mark and, sometimes, may even be from lists earmarked for other cases.

One sign that you will have a hard time winning a case is when the opposing attorney, prior to going on the record, looks up at the judge and says, "Hi, Joe, how's the kids?" and the judge responds just as warmly.

Early Friday afternoons are a time for conferences at the bench. If you have ever watched a court proceeding, you will know that sometimes a judge will call the attorneys up to the bench where the three will whisper together for a few minutes. One typical conversation is as follows:

JUDGE: Look you guys, I have to get to my summer house by

five today. How much longer do you think this is going to take?

ATTORNEY 1: Well, after this witness, I have two more.

JUDGE: How much longer with this witness?

ATTORNEY 1: I should finish direct in ten minutes or so.

ATTORNEY 2: Cross should be about fifteen minutes.

JUDGE: Too long. Why don't we just put it over until Monday?

ATTORNEY 1: Fine with me, your honor.

ATTORNEY 2: OK with me. But could we put it over until Tuesday? I found this great fishing spot but I can only get there in a chartered plane. There's no return trip until Monday afternoon.

JUDGE: A fishing spot? Where?

Sometimes the conversations are more technical, as occur during a pennant race. Once, the conversation was never even held -- the judge merely stood up in the middle of a trial, walked back to his chambers, took off his robe, and then walked out of the courthouse to his waiting car. It was another fifteen minutes before the attorneys realized there was no judge.

Criminal Court

Many criminal court judges spend their lives campaigning to move to the civil side. For one thing, most cases in any given district will be criminal, which is bothersome due to overload. For another, criminal court judges have to do a lobster shift once a month. The lobster shift is night court, when arraignments are held.

Being a criminal court judge is also like being in a pressure cooker around the clock, not because of the nature of the work involved (which can be horrendous by itself), but because of forces at work that have nothing at all to do with the defendants (who all look alike after awhile anyway). These forces consist of A.D.A.'s, Legal Aid or similar defense contractors (such as 18-B's), and the administration.

Assistant District Attorneys represent the District Attorney in indicting and prosecuting defendants. Legal Aid or similar attorneys work by contract with the government to defend those prosecuted. A.D.A.'s have a good chance of moving on to a decent practice of law with a decent firm. Legal Aid or similar attorneys usually have little chance of moving on to something at a firm. Both groups are at times guilty of trying to push a judge into acting in a way that suits their purposes. If, for example, an A.D.A. is particularly obnoxious during a trial and eventually goes overboard against the repeated warnings of the judge, the judge might, within his powers, hold that lawyer in contempt. What happens next is that all of the A.D.A.'s on the floor will rush into the courtroom and start protesting. These lawyers swear that they will cause a slow down in that judge's courtroom, ensure that the office will refuse to prosecute any cases fielded out to him, and that they will throw eggs at his house on Halloween. Similarly, if a judge does the same with a Legal Aid attorney, all those attorneys will flood into the courtroom and make their threats.

Can these lawyers boycott a judge? Can they slow down the court proceedings? Of course they can. They can refuse to come up for bench conferences. They can concertedly file frivolous motions (this is criminal court, not civil, so there is no real sanction against frivolous motions). They can harass the judge and his clerk. They can write letters of denouncement to the mayor, the disciplinary committees, the Chief Judge of the district, the administrative judge -- they can make life miserable.

Are those actions befitting of a legal association of any kind? No; the actions are those of children rebelling against the father figure. A contempt citation can be immediately appealed; lawyers do it every day. But these lawyers sometimes want more -- they want the judge to side with them philosophically, to smile at them when they enter the courtroom (and not the other side), to stroke them, to let them control the courtroom and the proceedings.

It is true that criminal court judges seem to break down entirely every now and then. Such as when one judge brought an avowed murderess, on trial before him, to his home to spend the evening before the crackling fireplace. Or when a judge had a prostitute sit on his lap during calendar call.

The administrative judge, however, is the person who wields the real power. He can force a judge to kneel and beg forgiveness. The AJ handles how cases are farmed out, and where the lower court judges sit. He can, for example, decide that the rural district needs more help, and ship up a city judge whom he dislikes. And keep him there, and keep him there, and keep him there, until the judge starts to believe he is a sheep.

As for cases, if the AJ's clerk is told that a certain judge is to receive only petty larceny cases, while another is to receive the big cases which will bring publicity and an appointment or nomination to a higher judgeship, then that is what happens.

Justice is not blind; it's just a constant political battle.[5]

SEX REDUX

For those of you who did not believe the previous anecdote about judges and sex, I thought I might quote from portions of a report involving the threatened suspension and removal of a Surrogate Judge. The matter is titled, In the Matter of the Proceeding Pursuant to Section 44, subdivision 4, of the Judiciary Law in Relation to BERTRAM R. GELFAND, Surrogate, Bronx County, and was reported in the New York Law Journal, March 27, 1987.

The following excerpts have been edited to remove paragraph numbers and other irrelevant side-comments.

"Irene Gertel was employed by respondent [the judge] as a law assistant on his court staff. ... Respondent and Ms. Gertel had a sexual relationship from September, 1978 to Aug. 2, 1985. ... In December, 1980, respondent was confronted about the sexual affair by Ms. Gertel's husband, who threatened to inform respondent's wife about the affair. Respondent told Ms. Gertel's husband that the affair was over. ... In May, 1984, respondent accused Ms. Gertel of having sexual relations with other men. Respondent requested and accepted Ms. Gertel's resignation because of his anger and jealousy ... The sexual relationship between respondent and Ms. Gertel continued during the period she worked at MHIS. While she worked at MHIS, respondent accused Ms. Gertel of having an affair with a doctor ... In September, 1984, respondent decided to rehire Ms. Gertel ... In October, 1984, respondent accompanied Ms. Gertel on a visit to her psychiatrist. Respondent told the psychiatrist that Ms. Gertel had been lying to the psychiatrist about her relationships with other men. Prior to visiting the psychiatrist, respondent drafted, and had Ms. Gertel sign, an agreement whereby she would be liable to him for $100,000 if she revealed to anyone that he had accompanied her to the session. ... During the weekend of July 19, 20 and 21, 1985, respondent learned that Ms. Gertel had been dating and having sexual relations with Steven Kessler, an Assistant District Attorney in Bronx County. Respondent confronted Ms. Gertel about this affair, and she confirmed it. ... Because of jealousy, respondent immediately demanded Ms. Gertel's resignation ... On July 23, 1985, respondent summoned Ms. Gertel and Mr. Kessler to his chambers. Respondent told Mr. Kessler that he knew of his relationship with Ms. Gertel and repeatedly denigrated Ms. Gertel, calling her a "whore," a "slut," a "bitch ..." ... Respondent ... told Mr. Kessler to "stay away" from her. ... Respondent ... began leaving obscene and annoying messages on Ms. Gertel's answering machine. ... Later ... respondent ... entered Ms. Gertel's office. Respondent ... took various personal items from Ms. Gertel's desk, cabinet and walls and put them into two boxes. [He] then drove to Ms. Gertel's home and left the boxes on her porch. ... [R]espondent also left numerous offensive messages on Mr. Kessler's answering machine. ... Respondent ... also placed calls to Ms. Gertel's roommate, her roommate's father, a friend, Ms. Gertel's brother and Mr. Kessler's grandmother in attempts to reach Ms. Gertel. ..."

The judge continued his harassment even after the relationship had been ended, including trying to keep the woman from any employment related to the law. During the proceeding, the judge attempted to wave the entire matter away.

Cloaking one's mania behind robes reminds me of those politicians and evangelists who always rant about abortions, homosexuals and liberals. For some reason, they're always caught with their pants down in the bathrooms of train stations.

Footnotes:

1. This exaggeration is not far from the truth. Article I judges are those people who are appointed to preside at legislatively created "courts" or regulatory tribunals. Up until the early 1980's, for example, regulatory judges were not permitted to wear judicial robes to hearings. They wore suits. Then it was decided that they could wear judicial robes. What robes have to do with justice has never been explained, just as it has never been explained why lawyers have to wear three-piece suits. In some states, such as California, it is not unusual to see attorneys appearing in court dressed in blue jeans and brightly colored shirts open to belly buttons. Robes do look impressive, however, and can double as tents on camping trips.

2. A difference between a semi-judge and a real judge is often a concept known as life tenure. On some courts, a real judge, once appointed, can remain a judge for as long as he likes, doing just about whatever he likes. A semi-judge, on the other hand, must be reappointed at intervals. This explains not only why real judges are better people, better judges, and greater intellects than semi-judges, but also why real judges are paid substantially more.

3. If the use of marijuana in the 1960's or 1970's is now a cause for denying a judgeship, it is likely that one generation of legal minds will never have a single judge appointed from it.

4. Wealthier individuals who have creditor problems because they have bought too many airplanes, cars, or mansions file for bankruptcy relief under Chapter 11 of the Bankruptcy Code, which was conceived of as a business reorganization chapter. These debtors appear in court wearing expensive suits and are represented by a battery of attorneys.

5. It is well known that judges who remain on a lower state bench for any length of time are eventually driven insane. On the criminal side, the same defendants are brought in day after day represented by the same lawyers and prosecuted by the same A.D.A.'s. The lawyers snipe at each other. The judge snipes at the lawyers. The defendant's family snipes at everyone. Even the clerks and guards become involved. The sniping is all preparatory to one of the lawyers announcing that he is not yet prepared, or needs a new trial date because he is on trial elsewhere. It's unusual for a criminal court judge to get a case that wakes him up. For example, People v. Nikki G. Craft, 134 Misc.2d 121 (City Court of Rochester 1986), involved a violation of New York Penal Law section 245.01, forbidding women to publicly reveal "that portion of the breast which is below the top of the areola."

Some women bared themselves to test the law. One of their arguments was that men were permitted to go topless. The judge wrote, "Although the public exposure of men's breasts may be unpalatable to some, society, acting through its Legislature, has decided that such exposure is not so offensive as to require prohibition." Meanwhile, a New Jerseyan, Michael Case, killed his IBM PC and color monitor by firing his .44 magnum automatic at them. Police Lt. Donald Van Tassel reported that Case was shocked at being arrested. "He couldn't understand why he couldn't shoot his own computer in his own home." And when pesticide companies spray the lawns of Wauconda, Illinois, they must post a sign reading, "This lawn is chemically treated," or be in violation of the village ordinance. So even the interesting cases seem to have something wrong with them, as if they had been directed by Rod Serling.

CHAPTER FOURTEEN

ETHICS

Lawyers are supposed to be guided by ethical considerations even to the point of not breathing if it might give an "appearance of impropriety." As among themselves, of course, lawyers will do everything unethical they can devise if it will help them on their path toward the paradise of partnership or vice presidency.

But then, the code of ethics (or professional responsibility) is not geared toward the behavior of lawyers among themselves. The code is a public relations device aimed at making lawyers look decorous and above-board to the general public, consisting of potential clients. For actual clients, the code provides tremendous discretion to an attorney as to whether or not to tattle-tale on a client who is contemplating unlawful actions.

In other words, the ethical umbrella of the law castigates ambulance chasing, most advertising, and cat calls in open court. Even so, it is extremely difficult to bring disciplinary proceedings against an attorney and harder still to triumph.

Ambulance Chasing

Let's look at the ambulance chasing/advertising situation first. Lawyers, for years, were never permitted to do either, on the surface. Lawyers, of course, have always ambulance chased and advertised. When Charlie the lawyer is at a party, he is going to tell everyone he is a lawyer and hand out numerous business cards. When Buffy is swimming at the pool, she will pull cards from her waterproof bra. When Harvey reads in the Wall Street Journal that so and so has been promoted to President at X Corporation, he is going to drop him a congratulatory note on the firm's letterhead. When Marv

215

transfers between firms, he is going to drop notes to all his former clients. When Ginny leaves her government position to join a firm as a partner, the firm is going to send out expensive engraved announcements. In fact, all firms maintain mailing lists, composed of the names of other lawyers, actual clients, former clients, family, friends, and the town drunk and his pet goldfish.

The above has never been considered ambulance chasing/advertising.

Referrals

Another route involves referrals. This can occur within a firm or between firms or among firms in different states. When the corporate department is approached by a client who says he wants to sue for breach of contract (because the corporate department did not draft a comprehensive contract and/or the contract did not provide

---

ON REFERRALS

When a lawyer or law firm refers a matter to another lawyer or law firm, the referral is supposed to be for the benefit of the client. Unless the referring lawyer has already done a lot of work on the case, or will be contributing substantially to the progress of the case, there should be no payment required to that lawyer or firm.

Except that in many cases a payment is expected as a matter of course. If a lawyer does not kick back some money (usually forty to fifty percent of the gross), he will soon discover that he no longer gets referrals.

Sending a thank you note, chocolates, or flowers is never thought sufficient.

---

for less expensive settlement techniques), the corporate department, of course, "refers" the matter to the litigation department.

If the firm does not have a litigation department, a partner may refer the matter to a former classmate of his at another firm. In return, the partner will get a portion of the fee. In every walk of life other than the law that arrangement is known as a "kickback."

If the lawsuit has to be in another state, the partner will hire local counsel (because of lack of reciprocity and local court rules) and everyone will get their share in the consolidated bill sent to the client. In return, local counsel will hire the partner when he needs representation in that partner's state. In every walk of life other than the law, that arrangement is known as "the payoff."

A client, of course, has little alternative other than to follow his lawyer's advice as to whom he should use. Service organizations, such as bar associations, are usually not permitted to advise people as to who is the recommended attorney in terms of particular matters. Or the least expensive. Potential clients are given an all-inclusive "list" of attorneys or referred to the yellow pages. That means calling an attorney who will either take on the case or "refer" it.

Advertising Expertise

Attorneys also "advertise their expertise" through lectures at seminars, writing articles and books, and joining bar association committees. I term this advertising because, in most instances, the lawyer does not know what he is talking or writing about, even though he has published and lectured·extensively on one topic.

A good example is computer law. That area of the law, not yet recognized by the legal community (i.e., it has not been graced with a West key number), is a "hot" area because almost everything that occurs today involves hardware, software, or enhanced communications. The industry itself is extremely complicated and requires a sophisticated understanding of electronics, transmissions, facilities, configurations, and of select words, such as bit and byte. The law as it stands today accommodates none of those aspects.

Few lawyers are going to master technology. Instead, they will lecture and write about computer law, relying on "normal" law and stating vociferously that that is all one needs to know to become an expert. One of the more hilarious events is to attend a prestigious seminar on "computer law" and sit through two days of people speaking about nothing.

WHAT DOES IT TAKE TO BE DISBARRED?

Disciplinary boards more often than not will warn or suspend an attorney. Disbarment is considered an extreme penalty. It is usually reserved for powerful lawyers whom everyone has hated for years but had to wait to attack until they are on the verge of death. A recent example is Roy Cohn, who was counsel to Mc-Carthy during that infamous era, and then became influential in politics and, supposedly, with criminal figures. After waiting for thirty years, the disciplinary committee attacked him as soon as it became known that he was dying of AIDs.

Here's another example of what one has to do to be disbarred. It was reported as In the Matter of Leroy Hodge, 116 AD2d 844 (3d Dep't 1986).

" ... The first charge of professional misconduct ... accuses respondent of violating the Code of Professional Responsibility ... by participating in the development and implementation of a scheme to launder the cash proceeds of illicit narcotics sales.

" ... [R]espondent "intended to implement a scheme to convert and channel cash derived from an illicit source into legitimate financial channels where it could surface without detection of its nature" in violation of Federal law and that respondent "believed, in accepting substantial sums of money from Federal

---

More Ways Of Sucking In Clients

Bar associations serve as central activity places where lawyers can get together, hobnob, drink, pretend to be erudite, and whisper about specialties, referrals, and kickbacks. I remember one partner insisting upon a certain matter being referred to a potential mistress of his who had no background at all in the particular area at issue. But they both belonged to the same bar association.

---

agents, and purchasing bearer bonds as a coverup, he was converting money derived from drugs." ...

"... Respondent has pleaded guilty to a Federal felony ... Also, it appears respondent entered into the scheme solely for pecuniary gain and expected a long-term business relationship with the other participants. Moreover, this is not the first time respondent has been disciplined by this court. In 1968 respondent was suspended for four months for neglect of clients' affairs, conversion of escrow money, breach of a settlement agreement, and making various misrepresentations to clients and fellow attorneys ...

"While we acknowledge some mitigating circumstances favoring leniency, including letters ... attesting to respondent's good character and reputation in his community, that no client has suffered because of his criminal activity, that respondent has already endured ... adverse newspaper publicity, and that he eventually cooperated with Government prosecutors ... we nevertheless conclude that in order to maintain the public's confidence in the system of attorney discipline and to protect the public from an attorney willing to participate in serious criminal activity, the ultimate sanction of disbarment is appropriate."

Question: Acknowledge what? Eventually cooperated? Ultimate sanction? How much has this guy squirreled away in Switzerland?

219

What You Aren't Supposed To Know ...

In recent years, lawyers have been permitted the luxury of tasteful advertising. Considering the nature of our society and its dependence upon media advertising, the fact that most law firms still do not advertise other than in the manner described above shows that it has been found to be an extremely successful form of bringing in financially secure clients.

There are exceptions. Some sole practitioners advertise in newspapers and subways, promising personal bankruptcies at $100, uncontested divorces for $75, simple wills for $50, and so on. When a matter becomes contested, either the fee goes up or the attorney withdraws.

I have been involved in a number of flat fee cases where the other side folded and settled as soon as I appeared to argue the matter. In one, the judge actually lambasted the attorney for advertising low fees and attaining a case load he obviously could not handle. But I believe that the advertising serves a useful purpose. In many of the cases, the plaintiff would never have gone to court and would have ended up at the mercy of threatening forces represented by pinstriped attorneys. At least the low cost attorney provides some breathing space for the poorer fellows around, especially where the issue is one that cannot be resolved pro se in a small claims' court.

Moreover, most matters can be resolved for a small fee. As already discussed, much of the law depends upon certain forms. Those forms are available at legal stationers, in form books, or in software packages. The vast majority of wills, the vast majority of separation agreements, the majority of contracts, all incorporation papers, most partnership papers, all powers of attorney, most shareholder agreements, and all UCC filings can be completed using simple forms.

Because of that reality, franchise firms are beginning to spring up providing low cost legal services from shopping malls and corner stores. Such firms are taking advantage of media advertising, including television spots. And they are being attacked in courts and in the press as undermining the ethics of the law.

Let me emphasize again (lawyers always emphasize things again because it adds billable time), that the concerns with ambulance

YOU CANNOT PRACTICE LAW UNLESS YOU ARE ETHICAL

Remember Rosemary Furman? She was 57 years old, a stenographer, a person who was angry that lawyers charged so much for simple filings, such as for uncontested divorces, adoptions, and name changes.

So she put together kits explaining how those could be done by a person without a lawyer.

The Florida bar association immediately lodged a complaint that she was practicing law without a license. After a hearing, she was ordered to go to jail and pay $7,802 in court costs.

She was eventually given a reprieve.

Curiously, bar associations don't lodge complaints against everyone who practices law without a license. One group involves literary and film agents, who negotiate contracts for their clients and append form clauses.

Another group includes publishing houses and software developers who market forms available to the public.

---

chasing/advertising are laughable. If it is done flagrantly behind the scenes, why not do it flagrantly? Society will adjust to it the way it sees fit.

Much has been made of the fact that law-services' television advertising increased from $900,000 in 1978 to $56 million in 1987, with the Jacoby & Meyers franchise heading the list ($6.4 million in 1987). Toward the end of March, 1988, Jacoby & Meyers released a $6.5 million campaign which included endorsements from partners at two large prestige firms. At the same time that various bar associations were contemplating flinging the wrath of God upon the J&M heads, one of my clients received a letter from a presitigous firm which declared, "it would be better if some of these law firms [which advertise] spent more time studying the law ... and less time becoming experts in marketing." Frequently, the letter went on, this firm which does not advertise is asked by clients of firms which do advertise to take on their cases, but it is often "too late to help." The letter closes with a thank you for referrals of new clients.

Only a lawyer would argue that the firm's letter denigrating firms which advertise was not itself an advertisement -- and one which blatantly hit below the belt by suggesting that cases handled by those other firms would end up being losers. What's even more ironic about this situation is that advertising by lawyers was not banned until 1908, and it took until 1976 for a couple of lawyers to realize that the right to free speech guaranteed by the First Amendment of the United States Constitution might possibly apply to lawyers.

If some lawyers want to run ads with half naked women draped over content clients, why not? Other ads which have brought the ire of local bar associations include a dom. rel. firm that showed a couch being sawn in half, and a criminal law lawyer promising bicycles to clients whom he couldn't get off scot-free from a drunken driving charge. Some people want that kind of lawyer. If some lawyers want to run special family discounts (wills and divorces for all), why not?

Advertising is not going to lower the esteem of lawyers in the public eye because that esteem is already non-existent. If lawyers want to raise their PR ratings, let them clean their own houses first.

Fee And Frivolity

To further investigate this absurdity known as legal ethics, move over to the world of no fee splitting with a layman. That code section supposedly prevents a lawyer from entering into an arrangement with a non-lawyer where income from the practice of law is shared with the non-lawyer. What's funny about it is that, if you think it through, lawyers would be unable to purchase anything, since all their money comes from fees. This section has been applied to prevent an attorney from entering into a percentage lease in an area where all office space was being rented on a percentage basis. The fear was that the landlord might interfere with the lawyer's practice.

One can imagine the landlord standing behind the attorney and kibbitzing. "Take that client. Don't take that client. Why'd you charge him only a hundred? He would have paid at least three hundred. Trust me. I know these guys."

Yet no one squeals when an attorney takes on a case from the slumlord who has not provided services to his tenants for years, has been in tax arrears for years, and the only purpose for the suit against the city is to contest the city's tax claims -- an utterly frivolous suit since the tax regulations and facts are clear -- and/or to enjoin the city from proceeding to foreclosure. Do ethics committees come swooping down with the American flag flapping overhead and the sound of martial brass thundering and condemn the attorney?

The lawyer knows it is a frivolous suit brought to buy time for the landlord. And the landlord has the following rule of thumb: if you owe the city $X and have not paid it, you have $X in the bank collecting interest. As long as that interest pays your legal fees, continue the suit. As soon as the city's claim ($X plus interest) equals your principal plus interest, either settle or abandon the buildings.

Settlement and abandonment in this context means being judgment proof and taking the squirreled away $X to purchase another slum building. Who set up the dummy corporations, made the landlord judgment proof, and perpetuated the frivolous suits? The lawyer. The same lawyer who rants and raves about law firm franchises advertising on television.

Is There Morality Involved?

Another interesting point about legal ethics is that often a truly personal, moral question will arise. Does one defend the Iranian government in this country with regard to loan claims, or bring suit for Iran on letters of credit payable here? Presumably a tough moral question, but there were and are a lot of firms out there, including Jewish firms, that would kill for the opportunity to have Iran as a client.

Instead of worrying about the moral implications of that kind of representation, some lawyers toss and turn at night wondering whether they are morally obligated to take on a pro bono case: permitting Nazis to march around; permitting white policemen to kill blacks; getting an admitted mass murderer off on a technicality. The intensity of these moral questions is such that one sometimes reads of attorneys running off with inmates. I don't know. I just wouldn't feel secure waking up next to someone wanted in fifty states.

Other true ethical questions: the female attorney told to defend the admitted violent rapist; the black attorney who has to represent the white policeman who overreacted during a ghetto riot; the Jewish attorney who has to represent the PLO.

These are real moral problems because the only reason those specific attorneys are ordered to defend those clients is strategic -- the impact on the jury. During a divorce, for example, the husband often switches from a male to a female attorney because of the subliminal effect of having a female attack a female.

A major ethical problem has been investments. The genetic attorney is attracted to a good inside deal like a bee to honey and, at his wedding, the presiding judge (attorneys are always married by judges) will discuss investments as a sacramental rite of passage to adulthood. Attorneys, ethically, are not supposed to do anything tainted with impropriety; by statute, attorneys are not supposed to use inside information for personal gain.

Law firms take this very seriously and send around thick memos that declare that attorneys are not to use inside information on clients for financial gain, such as buying stock right before the merger the firm is working on, or selling stock right before filing the annual report the firm is working on.

But that's about as far as it goes. Although it is true that most attorneys will not use inside information, it always seems that their close relatives are getting richer from investments.

What is curious about this aspect of self-policing is that lawyers caught with their hands in the cookie jar are always prosecuted first by the Securities and Exchange Commission and then disciplinary proceedings are brought against them. You never read about disciplinary proceedings being brought first.

What about the lawyer who steals away clients from a former firm and destroys the reputation of his former co-partner and associates just for the heck of it? Is he disciplined? At most, the former firm will sue him over billings.

What about the female client who makes love to a partner so that he will shave the bill or not bill at all?

What about the associate who continues to work on a major case for months until he learns through the grapevine that the partner had settled it? The client will be billed for that time anyway.

What about the law firm that sends around a memo to its support staff, assuring them of certain bonuses and salary increases at the end of the year and then, at the end of the year, "re-construing" the memo to make both discretionary, thereby not granting either?

What about lawyers in medical malpractice cases who hire expert witnesses based upon those witnesses agreeing (for a fee) to testify in a manner slanted to the lawyer's side? Or who prep a plaintiff to creep, stagger, limp into court while wearing an unnecessary neck brace?

What about the partner who has illegitimate children by his various secretaries? Do you ever read about him being marched before an ethics committee? Of course not, because no one will cast the first stone. Lawyers know that if they really begin policing themselves, all hell will break loose.

What about the lawyers who feed on a personal instability? A client dies. The only asset in the estate is the client's copyright to a book that is not bringing in royalties anymore. The client's bereaved widow makes an appointment to see the attorney. He graciously waives a consultation fee. She is in her late sixties, living on social security. She says to the attorney that she has no idea what she is to do, but perhaps the copyright has some value. She knows that her husband had been approached over the years by people who seemed interested in purchasing it, although she is not sure why. She knows nothing of such matters.

The attorney pats her shoulder and says he will see what he can do. Of course, he is quite aware of the copyright and of the sale possibilities, because he handled the initial negotiations. Instead of telling her to go to a literary agent, who gets a ten to twelve percent cut of residual sales of rights, he hems and haws and says: "I'll tell you what. I'll make some time to see what I can do with this. But because I'll be putting my own time and money into the effort, the best thing would be for me to just buy the rights from you. That way, you have money up front and, if I can't do anything with the copyright, I'm the loser, not you." She gladly takes the twenty thousand dollars he offers and toddles off.

The lawyer knows that even if he loses out, he will have a nice deduction, but he also knows that he will not lose out. This is, after all, a lesson in ethics and naivete. From the prior negotiations, the lawyer already is aware of a demand for the copyright for a movie sale. He would not plunk down his money unless he had someone he could turn to that day for an immediate turnover. And, indeed, he does, selling the film rights for a quarter of a million dollars. Not a bad profit.

There is no reason to dwell on this much more, because all one will come up with is more nonsense. The lawyer who will not succeed will know what I am talking about; the genetic lawyer will merely shake his head and grin. Unfortunately, grins on the mouths of genetic lawyers are not quite as attractive as those on Cheshire cats. If the latter grin enough, they disappear.